TEMPTATION

Dealing With Temptation, Test & Trial

A Guide For Believers

Revised Edition

Pastor David Amoah

Temptation

Unless otherwise indicated, all Scripture quotations are taken from the *New International Version* of the Bible, Copyright © 1973, 1978, 1984, The International Bible Society. Used by permission.

All scripture quotations marked (KJV) are taken from the *King James Version* of the Bible.

All scripture quotations marked (NKJV) are taken from the *New King James Version* of the Bible, Copyright © 1979, 1980, 1982, Thomas Nelson, Inc. Used by permission. All rights reserved.

Scripture quotations marked (NLT) are taken from the *Holy Bible New Living Translation* of the Bible, Copyright © 1996, 2004 by Tyndale Charitable Trust. Used by permission of Tyndale House Publishers.

Originally published 2010 by In the Way Publishing, London

ISBN 978-1-907654-04-6

1st Printing 2010

This edition published 2015 by Life and Success Media Ltd

E-mail: info@lifeandsuccessmedia.com

www.lifeandsuccessmedia.com

Copyright ©2013 David Amoah

E-mail David Amoah

amoahdla@yahoo.co.uk

Find out more about David Amoah at: www.davidamoah.org

ISBN Number: 978-1-907402-78-4

All rights reserved. No part of this publication may be produced, distributed, or transmitted in any form or by any means, including photocopying, recording or other electronic or mechanical methods, without prior written permission of the publisher, except in the case of brief quotations embodied in critical reviews and certain other non-commercial uses permitted by copyright law.

For permission requests, write to the publisher, addressed "Attention:

Permissions Coordinator" at the email address above

Dedication

Once again I dedicate this book, the Revised Edition of my first fruit 'Lead Us Not Into Temptation' to the Almighty God and Lord of all who gives me the knowledge, courage and the materials through the leading of the Holy Spirit to write books.

***

Contents

Foreword 7

Preface 11

The Purpose And The Theme Of This Book 15

The 'Temptation Phenomena' 19

'Temptation Defined' 25

The 'Opportunity' In Temptation 31

Preparing For Temptation 35
1. 'Be self-controlled' (1 Peter 5:6) 37
2: 'Be alert' (1 Peter 5:8) 41
3: 'Resist Satan' (1 Peter 5:9) 44
4: 'Stand firm in Faith' (1 Peter 5:9) 47
5: 'Be prepared to suffer a little while' (1 Peter 5:10) 50

Temptation, Test Or Trial 53

The Tests Or Trials Of God 57
The Lord tested Abraham 59
The Lord tried the Israelites 61
The Lord tested the woman at Zarephath 62
Jesus tested the faith of the Canaanite woman 64
The Temptation of Job 66

The Temptations of the Devil 69
Our Weaknesses 70

Our Evil Desires 71
Our Doubt 72
Our Disobedience 76

How To Be Successful In Temptation, Test And Trial .. 81
The Adam & Eve Method 84
The David Method 88
The Abraham Method 95
The Job Method 103
The Joseph Method 115
The Jesus Method 120

Joyful In Temptation 131

Conclusion 143

Other Publications by Pastor David Amoah 147

Foreword

More than fifteen years of teaching, preaching and deliverance ministry in the service of Our Lord and Saviour Jesus Christ has made me fully aware of the challenges many Christians face on the issue of temptations, test and trials. In most case, people misunderstand the origins of their temptations and fail to handle them in victorious ways. They give in and see themselves as victims instead of handling those temptations proactively in order to emerge stronger and glorious from them. However, as a Pastor, I am also fully aware of how some Christians are able to handle temptations that come their way and emerge stronger in their faith. I have witnessed people overcoming Satan and living victorious lives afterwards. The fact is whether we like it or not, there is a constant battle between making the right choices over wrong ones. God has graciously endowed all His children with power to overcome temptations to the shame of Satan.

As I have taught and preached on the topic of temptations, tests and trials for so many years, I commend Pastor David Amoah, who is a long-time friend and partner in ministry, for his dedication in teaching and meticulous work on the subject, which is very central in the life of every Christian. I strongly believe in and support his ministry. So when he called upon me to do the foreword of this great guide book on temptations, I did not hesitate at all because I know him personally, I know the kind of person he is and the anointing of the Lord upon his life and ministry.

Pastor David Amoah, having been taught and trained as a true man of God proclaiming the unadulterated word of the Lord and walking in the footsteps of Jesus, more than qualifies to write such a manual on temptations and trials and has comprehensively and ably treated the subject for the maximum benefit of all readers. This book will therefore be very resourceful to all persons because it exposes, teaches and explains practical ways of handling what I term -Triple Ts (Temptations, Tests, and Trials).

After having discussed the true biblical foundations of temptations, test and trials, the book guides readers to know the differences between temptations from Satan, the test and trials from God and their different purposes in the life of a Christian. My dear friend, in this book, you will also be taught and encouraged, with biblical examples, of how not to only endure but to enjoy "opportunities" in temptations because after you have emerged from it, you will obtain greater reward and many spiritual benefits.

Pastor David Amoah eloquently demonstrated successful methods of dealing with temptations and trials in this book such as what he terms the "Abraham Method", the "Job Method", the "Joseph Method" and the "Jesus Method" – thereby contrasting such methods with the other unsuccessful methods used by Adam and Eve, and David. All methods are worth knowing when facing trials and temptations.

While it is quite clear from this book that temptations are inevitable and are bound to come the way of men and women, the author continue to makes it absolutely clear too on Biblical principles that they must not overcome a child of God. Through vigilance, prayer and by the power of God, the follower of Christ becomes a resister of the devil through the Word.

Without any iota of doubt in my mind and heart, this book would be beneficial to every believer, church members, church leaders and the youth as a lasting manual that can serve as a reference in the understanding of and dealing with temptations, test and trials. I am absolutely convinced that by buying and utilising this book, there is no way a child of God will not be able to overcome temptations, test and trials no matter how cunning the trap of Satan becomes. Enjoy reading it and be sure to get a copy for a friend for in life good things are meant to be shared.

Apostle Dr. Justice Kofi Annan
(General Overseer, Destiny Apostolic Church International, London)
London, November 2013

***

Preface

I truly believe that the life of a Christian – a born-again believer and follower of Jesus Christ – is the most wonderful and fulfilling life a person can have. However, I also know that the life of a Christian is not necessarily an easy or straightforward one as many people think, it is not always bread and butter there are challenges.

As Christians, we benefit immeasurably from the fact that our Saviour has redeemed us from the curse of the law: redeemed us from sickness, disease, iniquities and eternal death. That is, Christ performed the 'finished work' on the Cross for us that, in our weakness as mere human beings, we could never hope to have performed and can never hope to improve upon.

The very fact that we are human beings, and not heavenly ones, with bodies that have a wide range of physical and emotional needs and desires; means we face the constant challenge of having to work on our salvation with 'fear and trembling' (Philippians

2:12); on a day-to-day and often moment-to-moment basis.

This is true of every, Christian, great or small, newly born again or mature in the Lord! We all have to work at living lives that are pleasing to Christ, lives that bring Him honour and glory. As Christians, one of the main and most powerful challenges we are confronted with, is the very real and ever present challenge of the 'temptation to sin'.

In this book Revised Edition of my first book 'Lead us Not into Temptation I aim to expand on some of the topics discussed in the first edition. I add that in order to be victorious over temptation and lead a life that pleases our Maker, and satisfies ourselves and others; there is every need for us to continually look unto Jesus the author and finisher of our faith (Hebrews 12:2). He has the answer to every challenge that we may face in life so long as we abide in Him or stay connected to Him. He is not only the reason for our faith; He is also the image (example) of it and should be its focus.

It is my prayer as you progress through the pages of this guide that you will come to accept that Jesus Christ truly is the way, the truth and the life in all things (John 14:6) including, being and providing the solution to the ever present life challenges of temptation, test and trial.

***

The Purpose And
The Theme Of This Book

There is a prevailing belief among many believers, and even some preachers preach that once a person accepts Jesus Christ as Lord and Saviour; and thus becomes born again – he or she is free from temptation. This is a misled conception that has left many believers confused and others disappointed because after their salvation they found that message to be untrue. There are others also who have the view that temptation is a form of punishment from God, and therefore is impossible to overcome.

In the pages of this book to deal with the phenomena of 'temptation, test and trial', I aim to demonstrate through the Word of God that, temptation is an ever present part of life whether you are Christian or not. I will also prove that temptation (test and trial from God and temptation that come from the Devil can be successfully managed by the grace of God.

It is important to know from the outset that temptation will come irrespective of your spiritual backgrounds, your relationship with God, and whether or not you deserve the 'punishment of temptation or the test of it'. Just as is the case with people today, we read of many people in the Bible who, were tempted; including our Lord Jesus Himself. We are all vulnerable to be tempted. For this reason in Luke 17:1, Jesus said to His disciples,

"There will always be temptations to sin" NLT

In 1 Peter 4:12, Peter advises us that trials are to be expected. He said:

"Dear friends, do not be surprised at the painful trial you are suffering, as though something strange were happening to you."

So do not be surprised when you are tempted. With the right knowledge to hand, temptation, in all its forms can be overcome. The challenge is, to recognise when we are being tempted, know what to do about it when we are, and take our stand against it.

Tragically, many have missed God's blessings and others have fallen into the Devil's hands because they failed to recognise the hour and the source of their temptation. Jesus told his disciples as recorded by Matthew in his book,

"Watch and pray so that you will not fall into temptation." Matthew 26:41

We should be aware that the existence of temptation is not sin in and of itself. We sin when we *'fall into'* temptation or give in to it. Jesus told His disciples to keep alert knowing that temptation will always strike where we are vulnerable.

In the pages of this guide, we'll take a closer look at one of the most important things about the subject of temptation, the phenomenon of temptation, *the differences between temptation, that which is from the Devil, test and trial, that which is from God, and how to handle them in order to become victorious.* It is very important for everyone to know the difference. Many fail to overcome temptation simply because they misjudge and blame God for temptation that comes from the Devil and others fail to successfully manage the test and trials that are from God because they think the Devil is the cause.

If you are currently facing temptation, test or trial, as you prayerfully read this book, I also pray that you will receive wisdom, strength and power from the Holy Spirit to help you to deal with it effectively. If you are not in the grip of any of these phenomena, at the moment, I pray that as you read you gain the information you need to prepare; so you can rise above and overcome temptation, tests and trials that *will* come your way in the precious name of Jesus Christ. Amen

***

The 'Temptation Phenomena'

The presence of temptation in a person's life is a mortal danger that should never be taken lightly. Not being able to withstand and correctly handle temptation can affect ones entire existence. As a result of giving in to and failure to discover the hour and the form of temptation, in any of its many forms, and properly dealing with it a person could lose their destiny, their blessings, their husband or wife, or any precious thing in a person's life, even their salvation could be in danger!

I believe that temptation has two sources. It can be an internal impulse, which wars within the heart, mind and soul of man; or it can be from an external evil influence, engineered by the Devil.

When, as Christians, we allow our desires and our weaknesses to have free course, when we let our impulses take control, when we succumb to temptations; we give place to the Devil as against the directive of scripture as Paul wrote in (Ephesians

4:27). Not to give Satan any glory, because he is the personification of evil. The evil impulse in natural man is something he thrives on, and uses against mankind, if he is given the chance, and if he gets the opportunity.

In Matthew 6:13,–He was fully aware of the dangers of temptation as recorded by the writer of Hebrews. "For in that He Himself has suffered, being tempted, He is able to aid those who are tempted." (Hebrews 2:18) when He was teaching them to pray Jesus said to His disciples, "When you pray tell your heavenly father and lead us not into temptation, but deliver us from the evil one."

This scripture is the foundation for this guide, the source of its title, and the key to the approach we must adopt in order to deal effectively with the phenomena of 'temptation'.

It goes without saying that temptation can be very difficult to handle. The 'temptation to sin' can range from the temptation to tell a 'white lie' to the temptation to murder another human being.

Whatever the source of temptation (within us or outside of us), temptation is always 'heard' or given audience in the heart and mind of man. This is why the Bible tells us in Proverbs 4:23,

"Above all else, guard your heart, for it is the wellspring of life."

The 'temptation to sin' can start as a nagging and persistent 'voice' encouraging us to do something we know we must not or should not do; with words like: "No one will know if I …" or "what harm can it do if I just …".

The Bible is full of warnings about this phenomenon. Here are a few examples:

"but each one is tempted when, by his own evil desire, he is dragged away and enticed. Then, after desire has conceived, it gives birth to sin; and sin, when it is full-grown, gives birth to death." James 1:14-15, and

"What causes fights and quarrels among you? Don't they come from your desires that battle within you?" James 4:1

Despite these truths, we should take comfort from 1 Corinthians 1:13 which says: "No temptation has seized you except what is common to man.

And God is faithful; he will not let you be tempted beyond what you can bear."

Hallelujah! As Christians, given that the Lord Himself has promised that He will not allow us to be tempted beyond our resistance levels – in every temptation we *should* be able to 'forbear'.

1 Peter 2:11 encourages us with these words:

"Dear friends, I urge you, as aliens and strangers in the world, to abstain from sinful desires, which war against your soul."

Contrary to what it may 'feel' like, when we are in it, we can take further comfort from the fact that the Lord is faithful to keep His Word that promises:

"I will not leave you nor forsake you", Hebrews 13:5, KJV and "I will be with him in trouble; I will deliver him and honour him", Psalm 91:15, KJV

Those who are able to endure periods of temptation, that is, 'bear up under it' will always experience the rewards of seeking God at this time. But, to be able 'bear up' we need to understand the nature of exactly what we are dealing with!

Before I move to define and examine temptation, and elaborate on "test and trial" to, distinguish the ways in which 'temptation' presents itself, and show how to handle these phenomena successfully; there is an important issue I want to uncover here.

In my role as Pastor of a church, I have observed many reactions like that of Job's three friends when they visited him in the time of his temptation. They said they believed the reason for Job's troubles was because he had sin and so they persuaded him to repent. I have heard many people say again and again; that they suspected the temptation they (or someone they knew) faced came as a result of their sins. The wrong concept that originates from the belief that bad things happens to bad people and good things happens to good people. I have also seen and heard of people, who, in the face of temptation lose all hope, blame God, and conclude that he has forsaken them.

These people believe it is the hand of God *only* when things are going well; and nothing to do with God in the times of suffering or difficulty! As we will see later in this guide – when God allowed Satan to tempt Job – temptation can be, but is not always, a result of our sins or mistakes; and that

God can allow us to be tempted by the Devil as it was in the case of Job!

***

'Temptation Defined'

Given that 'temptation' was specifically highlighted by Jesus in Matthew 6:13 as an 'evil' we must pray to the Father for help with – I believe knowing exactly what temptation really is – is critical. A study of the use of the word 'temptation' in the Bible will help us to recognise and understand it. As a result, I want you to pay extra attention to this part of the book for your understanding of this part will help you identify the source of any temptation that comes your way.

The Hebrew word for 'temptation' used forty times in the Old Testament is *'nasah'* (pronounced *'naw-saw'*). It literally means: 'to test', 'to try' and 'to prove', and refers to God *testing* the faithfulness of man in the Old Testament.

The words *'dokîmázô' and 'peirazô'* are Greek words used in the New Testament for 'temptation', 'trial' or 'test'. The specific use of either *'dokîmázô' or 'peirazô'* depends on the context in which either word is used in the Bible; and who is 'behind' the 'tempting'! Let me explain!

'peirasmos' from the root word *'peirazō'*, literally means putting to proof, to make trial of, try or tempt, and implies the trying of a person's character or virtues. *'peirasmos'* can be the 'solicitation to sin' from Satan – pure temptation; or a state of trial in which God brings His people through adversity and affliction to prove their faith in Him – a test or trial.

'dokîmázô' literally and figuratively means to test; and by implication it means to approve, allow, discern, examine or judge a thing to be fit and proper.

If it is God who is 'allowing' the tempting then it is *'dokîmázô'*. God can and may 'allow' His children to be 'tempted' to 'prove' us. In these instances the Lord is 'proving' us in the same sense as 'testing to determine if metal is pure'. This is a testing which aims at an ultimate spiritual good.

We see an example of the Lord's 'proving' of man in John 6:5-6. The Lord Jesus 'tried' Philip to 'prove' Philip's faith:

"When Jesus then lifted up his eyes, and saw a great company come unto him, he saith unto Philip, Whence shall we buy bread that these may eat?

And this he said to prove him: for he himself knew what he would do." KJV

Jesus is not testing Philip's ingenuity for, as we have just read, 'he (*Jesus*) himself knew what he would do'. He was instead 'challenging' Philip's faith, to bring Philip up higher. He was testing Philip's faith in His (the All Sufficient One's) ability to feed so many. Philip's answer: "Eight months' wages would not buy enough bread for each one to have a bite!" shows Philip is not exactly doubting, nor yet being fully persuaded that Jesus could feed the multitude.

Later in this book, we will see another example of the Lord's testing, when the Lord 'tried' and 'proved' Abraham's faith and obedience.

If it is the Devil tempting, then it is *'peirazó'*, the malevolent 'enticement to sin' form of *'peirazó'*; and is *definitely* for the purpose of evil! This is to say any attempt to entice or tempt into evil is from the devil. In tempting man, the Devil's main aim by 'solicitation to sin' is; convincing man to sin against God; and also to prove man's unworthiness. The Devil is determined to prove that man is evil, that he can be enticed to go against the will of God.

Ultimately, the purpose of the Devil's work, as the one who comes to 'steal, destroy and kill' (John 10:10) is to block the purpose of God being fulfilled in the lives of God's children. Satan is always the 'executor of temptation' that aims to lead man against the will of God; he is always behind its many faces!

Unfortunately for us, as I said in earlier, the Devil's temptations do not always look like a bad thing; it can come in very attractive wrapping! We need to be very, very careful not to be convinced that the Devil's temptation is a blessing, even an opportunity as it can be appealing.

The challenge is in distinguishing the test/trial that comes from the Lord and the temptation that comes from the devil. I will deal with how we make that distinction in more detail later under 'Temptation, Test or Trial?'

For now understand that the simplest way to distinguish the test/trial that comes from God, and the temptation which is from the Devil's is that – at the end of the Lord's test you will stand in righteousness and have divine approval, not condemnation. While at the end of every instance of Satan's temptations, is evil, sin and if we continue in it unrepentant, ultimately damnation!

But, even if it is the evil one who is tempting us, enticing us to sin, we can take comfort from the fact that what the Devil means for evil, God will turn around for our good (Romans 8:28). If we yield ourselves to Him, the Lord can use *every* temptation we face to 'try' man to, prove us good and acceptable. This is the 'opportunity in temptation' that I deal with in the next stage.

To conclude this part of the book this is how you can distinguish the temptation that is from the Devil and that which is from God:

1. Any attempt to entice or tempt a person into evil is from the Devil and
2. Also a testing which aims at an ultimate spiritual good for a person from God

***

The 'Opportunity' In Temptation

As I said earlier on, we are all susceptible to temptation. Scripture makes this clear. We need to know this truth so that we are not surprised or dismayed when it happens. Instead of being overwhelmed by the presence of temptation in our lives, we need to be vigilant; prepared for it.

As overpowering as temptation can be, I believe we can be on our way to defeating it, when we look to turn temptation into an opportunity. If we focus on the 'opportunity' temptation presents us to draw nearer to God, to strengthen our relationship with Him (the benefits of which I cover in more detail later in the chapter 'How to be Successful in Temptation, Test and Trial'), we are on our way to defeating it.

Our response to temptation then can signal that our 'hour of blessing' rather than our 'hour of doom' is upon us if not at hand. If we seek the Lord in our temptation, we will see the awesome Power of our

Lord in action. He will prove to us that we can rely totally on His wisdom and strength.

The good news is that the Bible tells us in Romans 5:3, when our faith is tested, it is a chance for our endurance to grow; and when our endurance is fully grown and developed, it produces strength of character that enables us to face any situation in life. Therefore, facing temptation can present us with the opportunity to grow in the Lord, to mature as Christians.

Temptation can also present us with the opportunity to learn about the nature of Satan's attacks and experience our 'faith tactics' at work. When we are able to bear or endure it, we become fully equipped in spiritual warfare against the wiles of the Devil.

Once we ourselves have been able to endure under temptation, I believe that we are then supposed to use our experience to turn back and help others who may also be tempted.

Jesus told Peter: "Simon, Simon, Satan has asked to sift you as wheat. But, I have prayed for you, Simon, that your faith may not fail. And when you have turned back, strengthen your brothers". Luke 22:31-32, NIV

As a Believer, when being tempted, tested or facing trials, it's not the time to panic, and not the time to run from God but a time to draw near and look to Him for the grace to turn temptation into an opportunity!

We will see later that when Christ faced temptation, He knew how to defeat it, and turn it into an opportunity to put Satan in His place! Since He Himself has gone through temptation and suffering, He is able to help us when we are being tempted. Hebrews 2:17-18, KJV states:

"For in that He Himself has suffered, being tempted, He is able to aid those who are tempted." Hebrews 2:18 (NKJV)

With Him, all things are possible (Luke 18:27). With Jesus every temptation, test or trial becomes manageable for no temptation is too big or too hard for Him to turn around, when we seek Him in it. Paul knew this secret when he said, "I can do all things through Christ who strengthens me" Philippians 4:13, NKJV

We too, like Christ, can turn the temptations we are confronted with into opportunities, when we handle them in God's way and with His help.

"My brethren, count it all joy when you fall into various trials, knowing that the testing of your faith produces patience. But let patience have *its* perfect work, that you may be perfect and complete, lacking nothing." James 1:2-4 (NKJV)

"Blessed *is* the man who endures temptation; for when he has been approved, he will receive the crown of life which the Lord has promised to those who love Him." James 1:12 (NKJV)

***

Preparing For Temptation

Now we understand what temptation is and are aware that it can present an opportunity as well as threat; we need to know how to be ready to turn this threat into opportunity. We need to be prepared for battle! Although as I have said the impulse to sin comes from within us, once it surfaces or is inflamed, our weaknesses become a battleground between the evil one and us.

Ephesians 6:12 warns us:

"For our struggle is not against flesh and blood, but against the rulers, against the powers of this dark world and against the spiritual forces of evil in heavenly realms".

'Spiritual forces of evil' are led by our known enemy, the 'accuser of the brethren' (Revelations 12:10). We know that the devil, in opposition to God's divine mission to bless His children, is at work 24/7 on his diabolic mission to damage (John 10:10).

The devil is dedicated to his purpose, he is never off duty! And so we must always be on guard. We read from Exodus 15:9:

"The enemy boasted, 'I will pursue, I will overtake them. I will divide the spoils; I will gorge myself on them. I will draw my sword and my hand will destroy them.'"

Also in Job 1:6 -7 we read:

"One day the angels came to present themselves before the LORD, and Satan also came with them. The LORD said to Satan, "Where have you come from?" Satan answered the LORD, "From roaming through the earth and going back and forth in it.""

'Temptation' is one of 'swords', the strategic weapons Satan draws on the battlefield of our hearts, minds and souls. As such, we need to be prepared with our own strategies.

Peter gives sound advice in 1 Peter 5:8-10:

"Be self-controlled and alert, your enemy the devil prowls around like a roaring lion looking for someone to devour. Resist him, standing firm in faith, because you know that your brothers throughout the world are undergoing the same kind of sufferings. And the God of all grace, who called you to his eternal glory in Christ, after you have suffered a little while, will himself restore you and make you strong, firm and steadfast."

I believe Peter's advice gives us six strategies we need to adopt, or actions we can use to prepare and stand in battle. We need to:

1. Be self-controlled (*1 Peter 5:8*)
2. Be alert (*1 Peter 5:8*)
3. Resist Satan (*1 Peter 5:9*)
4. Stand firm in faith (*1 Peter 5:9*), and
5. Be prepared to suffer a little while (*1 Peter 5:10*)

For clarity, let us take a closer look at each one in turn:

1. 'Be self-controlled' (*1 Peter 5:6*)

To discipline yourself or be self-controlled is when one is able to say no or to restrain himself from doing something despite the demand from his own body, from others or circumstances around him. This is when one is able to assert control not to yield to friends or any influence to do anything wrong that could harm oneself or others in the future. To discipline yourself or to exercise self-control is also when you refuse to watch what you love to because it is not good. Another way is being able to control the words that come out of your mouth; knowing when to speak and when to keep quiet.

Even though it is hard, to stop yourself from going after any man or woman who professes love for you, you need to be on guard against sexual temptation as you discipline yourself. Irrespective of the challenge it poses from your body and from others it is worth disciplining your emotions or exercising self-control.

As temptation can present itself at anytime, and when it does it can have a very, very powerful draw; we need to have our wits about us – at all times. We need to maintain control of ourselves; our thoughts, our emotions, our desires and our actions.

For us as Christians, self-control comes from having a regenerated heart and mind, focused on Christ, directed by the Holy Spirit; all to the glory of God the Father. When we read Ephesians 2, we find that our regenerated hearts and minds are a direct result of our becoming born again Believers.

'Self-control' is a 'gift' from God, 'gifted' to us on the point of salvation. It is one of the 'Fruits of the Spirit' named in Galatians 5:22-23, which we receive, on the point of salvation:

"But the fruit of the Spirit is love, joy, peace, patience, kindness, goodness, faithfulness, gentleness and self-control"

If we are born again Believers, in order to activate the fruit of 'self-control', we need to *do* something. We need to heed the advice the Apostle Paul gives in Romans 6:6 and 11-12:

"For we know that our old self was crucified with him so that the body of sin might be done away with, that we should no longer be slaves to sin … In the same way count yourselves dead to sin but alive to God in Christ Jesus. Therefore do not let sin reign in your mortal body so that you obey its evil desires."

Peter also advises in 1 Peter 4:1-3:

"Therefore, since Christ suffered in his body, arm yourselves also with the same attitude, because he who has suffered in his body is done with sin. As a result, he does not live the rest of his earthly life for evil human desires, but rather for the will of God. For you have spent enough time in the past doing what pagans choose to do – living in debauchery, lust, drunkenness, orgies, carousing and detestable idolatry."

Paul also advises in Galatians 5:16-18:

"... live by the Spirit, and you will not gratify the desires of the sinful nature. For the sinful nature desires what is contrary to the Spirit and the Spirit what is contrary to the sinful nature. They are in conflict with each other, so that you do not do what you want. But if you are led by Spirit, you are not under the law"

Ultimately, having self-control means being controlled by the Spirit of God. It is He who gives us power to control self; the resolve, to control ourselves and respond appropriately to temptation. 2 Timothy 1:7 says:

"For God did not give us a spirit of timidity, but a spirit of power, of love and of self-discipline."

Our gift of self-control is affected and strengthened, when we are in a constant state of prayer and fellowship with the Lord, through His Word. There are no easy options! When we have the knowledge of Him, when we meditate on His word day and night (Joshua 1:8); it is then that we are able to renew our minds and exercise the gift of self-control required to keep our hearts and minds (the battlefields of temptation), stayed on Christ!

2: 'Be alert' (*1 Peter 5:8*)

Unlike Paul, many people including believers are unaware of the ways of the enemy they are up against. As a result, sometimes they become self-confident and get carried away by complacency, forgetting that the Devil is at work 24/7. Friends, listen, we are fighting against someone we cannot see, someone who is very wicked and merciless. Paul said "… in order that Satan might not outwit us. For we are not unaware of his schemes," 2 Corinthians 2:11. It is only when you are alert and therefore aware of your enemy's scheme that you can confront or avoid his evil plans against you.

We have to be alert to our own weakness and to the wiles of the evil one. I said at the beginning of this chapter that the devil is never off duty! Knowing this we need to be alert, in a constant watchful state. As we have already read,

Matthew 26:41 says:

"Watch and pray so that you will not fall into temptation. The spirit is willing, but the body is weak."

'Being alert' literally means being in a watchful and prayerful state. Jesus Christ Himself says in Luke 21: 34-36:

"Be careful, or your hearts will be weighed down with dissipation, drunkenness and the anxieties of life, and that day will close on you unexpectedly like a trap. For it will come upon all those who live on the face of the whole earth, Be always on the watch, and pray that you may be able to all that is about to happen, and that you may be able to stand before the Son of Man." (See also Luke 22:40, 46)

1 Thessalonians 5:6 and 8 also gives sound advice on this to us as Believers, as 'children of light' (1 Thessalonians 5:5):

"Therefore let us not sleep, as do others; but let us watch and be sober ... But let us, who are of the day, be sober, putting on the breastplate of faith and love and for an helmet, the hope of salvation." KJV

We see echoes here of Ephesians 6:10-20, which we'll look at in point 4 below. Particularly relevant here though is Ephesians 6:18:

"Pray always with all prayer and supplication in the Spirit, watching thereunto with all perseverance and supplication for all the saints." KJV

We are literally to be physically and spiritually watchful against all those things that present a potential threat to us, and our brethren in the Body of Christ. Having identified the existence of a threat of temptation, we are to take our stand against it and pray.

Being alert is about action. Being mindful always of our weaknesses and the unseen enemy, who is at work non-stop, we must never let down our guard either:

"Lest Satan should take advantage of us: for we are not ignorant of his devices" 2 Corinthians 2:11, KJV

3: 'Resist Satan' (*1 Peter 5:9*)

So many people (both Christians and non-Christians alike) don't believe the existence of the devil, demons or evil spirits and therefore would not even talk about them. Others though believe they exist but take them lightly and least doing anything to resist. *Let me say this that I am not out to exalt the devil and his works but to reveal him and his evil plans to destroy mankind.*

Again there are two very real dangers I would like everybody to know when we are dealing with resisting Satan

1. There is the danger of **OVER ESTIMATING** his power and therefore we consequently get a defeatist attitude and inferiority complex
2. Also one can **UNDER ESTIMATE** the powers of Satan and this obviously will lead to complacency and a false security.

"Submit yourselves, then, to God. Resist the devil, and he will flee from you." James 4:7

Yes indeed, as James assures us when we resist Satan, he retreats. However, my brethren do not be fooled, that is not necessarily the end of the matter! We have to resist him continuously, without let up. Why? Luke 4:13, KJV tells us:

"And when the devil had ended all the temptation, he departed from him for a season."

The scripture is referring here to the temptation of our Lord Jesus Christ. Even though our victorious Redeemer stood his ground against Satan's persistent onslaught (which I will deal with later on in the book) when Satan retreated it was for a period of time *only*. He departed *'for a season'*. He retreated, but he did not resign!

The devil is exceedingly wicked; he does not make an exception for anyone, not even Jesus Christ. The devil does not have pity, mercy or respect; it is the nature of evil.

Matthew 12:43-45 tells us what happens when an unclean or evil spirit comes out of a man and then does not find another 'house'. It 'returns to the house it left'!

The 'evil one' will persistently tempt no matter who you are, what you are, or your circumstances. He *will* strike when he gets the opportunity.

The devil even likes to tempt us when we have received a miraculous breakthrough. He likes to tempt at this time because he knows that, as human beings, once we have obtained what we are seeking, we can become complacent and self-confident. Which is why we must be alert to our own failings too.

I can cite for you many instances of people I know who, when seeking a job, marriage, healing – you name it! – sought God fervently in prayer. They were the first person in church and studied the Word rigorously for direction and assurance. Once they received their answer, their prayer life and attendance slacked off. When questioned as to why, they made excuses.

Be careful my brethren! This is why Satan only leaves for a season, he is waiting for just such a *'fall'*, an unoccupied 'house', a moment of weakness, our over confidence; an opportune time.

I have also observed that temptation can be at its most persistent and strong when we are in one of those dark periods in life; going from crisis to crisis. Under pressure of circumstances, when our faith seems to fail us and we are at our most vulnerable, we can be easily tempted. Satan does not care whether you are already facing challenges or not, ill or in good health, rich or poor, man, woman or child; He *will* take advantage of any situation. However, praise God, for the next strategy and action!

4: 'Stand firm in Faith' (*1 Peter 5:9*)

Many times due to the intensity of our problems, we tend to think God has abandoned us and so we give up thinking that he does not even listen to our prayers and in extreme cases, it affects our relationship with God.

I would also like to admit that it is easy to give up and give in when things gets worse in life but whatever your situation may be I want you to know that God listens and hears the prayers of his children. Therefore my advice to you is: "never give up, stand firm on your prayer request"'PUSH' that is Pray Until Something Happens, for delay is not denial. Until you see the answer of your prayer request never stop praying and never think God does not hear you for delaying of answers to prayer have many reasons.

I love this part 'stand firm' and I pray it becomes as much of a weapon and a comfort to you, as it is to me. Ephesians 6:10-18 tells us to 'put on the full armor of God'. It is a comprehensive guide to standing firm in faith:

"Finally, be strong in the Lord and in his mighty power. Put on the full armor of God so that you can take your stand against the devil's schemes. For our struggle is not against flesh and blood, but against the rulers, against the authorities, against the powers of this dark world and against the spiritual forces of evil in the heavenly realms. Therefore put on the full armor of God, so that when the day of evil comes, you may be able to stand your ground, and after you have done everything, to stand. Stand firm then, with the belt of truth buckled around your waist, with the breastplate of righteousness in place, and with your feet fitted with the readiness that comes from the gospel of peace. In addition to all this, take up the shield of faith, with which you can extinguish all the flaming arrows of the evil one. Take the helmet of salvation and the sword of the Spirit, which is the word of God. And pray in the Spirit on all occasions with all kinds of prayers and requests.

With this in mind, be alert and always keep on praying for all the saints."

Praise His Name! The 'full armor of God' is not just for protection or defence, though it is for that too! When we put on the 'full armor of God', we are actually 'putting on Christ' Himself, His very nature.

To 'put on Christ' we subdue our weak flesh, 'die to self' to become alive to the nature of Christ. Putting on the 'full armour of God', 'putting on Christ' is about choosing to be sanctified and holy, not fulfilling the lusts of the flesh.

When 'we put on Christ', we choose to be Christ-like. We choose to be rooted in the Word of God; sanctified; walking in faith; armed with the Word of God; and prayerful doing the will of the Father, Amen!

Paul in his letter to the Romans writes:

"The night is nearly over; the day is almost here. So let us put aside the deeds of darkness and put on the armor of light. Let us behave decently, as in the daytime, not in orgies and drunkenness, not in sexual immorality and debauchery, not in dissension and jealousy. Rather, clothe yourselves with the Lord Jesus Christ, and do not think about how to gratify the desires of the sinful nature." Romans 13:12-14

When we are 'clothed' with Jesus Christ, we are fully equipped to defeat any temptation. Jesus Christ, the hope of Glory is able to defeat any temptation we may face. We have already read Philippians 4:13, NKJV which says: "I can do all things through Christ who strengthens me"

5: 'Be prepared to suffer a little while' (*1 Peter 5:10*)

Whenever you are prepared, nothing takes you by surprise. Being prepared or getting ready is a very good thing to do. It is a good foundation for everything in this life, especially things that concern spirituality, such as temptation. It is the key ingredient that makes any activity or eventuality successful. It is said that when preparation meets opportunity success is inevitable. This means that when you are prepared before temptation strikes you are more like to overcome than when not prepared.

No one likes to endure suffering, but, Philippians 1:29 makes it clear, that as believers, followers of Christ; we are to expect and embrace suffering:

"For unto you it is given in the behalf of Christ, not only to believe on him, but also to suffer for his sakes."

The Bible tells us that we must be 'prepared' (ready, set, equipped, geared up, organised) to 'glory in tribulations'. Romans 5:1-4, KJV:

"Therefore being justified by faith, we have peace with God through our Lord Jesus Christ: By whom also we have access by faith into this grace wherein we stand and rejoice in hope of the glory of God. And not only so, but we glory in tribulations also: knowing that tribulation worketh patience; and patience, experience and experience hope."

When you read 1 Peter 5:9 in full, note that we are not alone in our suffering. Other Believers, around the world, go through the same temptations, tests or trials we do! Not only that, believers in the past also faced and withstood temptation, test or trial. We should be encouraged by Hebrew 12:1, which says:

"Therefore, since we are surrounded by such a great cloud of witnesses, let us throw off everything that hinders and the sin that so easily entangles, and let us run with perseverance the race marked out for us."

We are preceded and surrounded by the Fathers of a faith, and many great people who came before us, fought the 'good fight of faith' and now surround us as a 'cloud of witnesses'.

1 Peter 5:10 goes on to assure us of what happens when we are prepared to 'glory in tribulations':

"In his kindness God called you to his eternal glory by means of Jesus Christ. After you have suffered a little while, he will restore, support, and strengthen you, and he will place you on a firm foundation." Amen!

We can have the strength, certainty and unwavering faith required to deal with temptation effectively, when we know these truths; and knowing these truths should help us to commit to preparing for temptation; and to stand in faith.

How far are you prepared to suffer for the sake of Christ knowing that suffering is inevitable as a Christian and a follower of Christ?

***

Temptation, Test Or Trial

Now we know how to prepare, we need to know exactly what we are preparing for! We need to know the nature of the temptation, tests or trials we are facing or could face in the future.

We have seen in 'Temptation Defined' that there are differing forms of temptation, test or trial. Knowing whether we are facing temptation (from the evil one), or a test or trial from the Lord, helps us know how to deal with it in the most appropriate way. In the face of what can all look and feels like 'temptation' we need to know the answer to the question 'am I facing temptation, test or trial?'

Due to their very nature, doubtless there are some temptations that are easily identifiable as such. Being tempted to steal, to kill or cause harm to someone, for example, can be easily identify as clearly Satan's temptations.

There are however some temptations whose true nature can be very, very difficult to identify. Why?

The Bible tells us that the Devil sometimes presents himself as an angel of light (2 Corinthians 11:14). He can present counterfeit opportunities that are 'temptations' in disguise.

We need wisdom from God to know the temptation that comes from the Devil and the test or trial that comes from God. In this regard, the advice of James in the Book of James 1:5 is appropriate:

"If any of you lacks wisdom, he should ask God, who gives generously to all without finding fault, and it will be given to him."

When we are faced with temptation of any kind, we must first go to God in prayer. What our Lord Jesus Christ, told His disciples to ask of the Father in prayer, in Matthew 6:13, is still true for us today, which is why I have made it the foundation for this guide. We need help from the Father to "deliver us from the evil one". We must always pray to Him to reveal to us the nature of what we are going through and how to handle it. So what am I teaching here? I want you to know as you read this book that if you face any situation of which you are not sure. Be it a temptation from the Devil that leads to destruction or a test or trial from the Lord that brings the

Lord's blessings, go to God in prayer. He will not only show you the originator of your situation but also show you how to deal with it.

***

The Tests Or Trials Of God

It is important to make it clear from the outset that the Lord Himself does not 'tempt'. This is a question many people wonder about and ask, 'Does God tempt man?' The answer is, God does not tempt, because He can never perform evil; and temptation is an evil.

"Every good and perfect gift is from above, coming down from the Father of the heavenly lights, who does not change like shifting shadows." James 1:17

I repeat God does not Himself tempt! James 1:13, makes it clear:

"Let no man say when he is tempted, I am tempted of God: for God cannot be tempted with evil, neither tempteth he any man." KJV

As I have said in 'Temptation Defined', God can and does allow Satan to tempt His people, but, as I've also said, this is not necessarily because He has forsaken or abandoned us nor is it His intention to see us destroyed but to prove us. The classic example of this is the temptation of Job, as we will see in more detail, later in this chapter.

God can and does allow us to face test or trial, not for evil purposes or intentions; or to allow Satan to have full reign over us. It is always to bless us when we are able to 'stand'! When we pass the test of God He always lifts us to the next level of our live.

The Lord knows what we can and cannot endure (remember He never gives us more than we can carry!). So, He will not allow us to be tempted beyond that which He knows we can bear. "No temptation has overtaken you except such as is common to man; but God *is* faithful, who will not allow you to be tempted beyond what you are able, but with the temptation will also make the way of escape, that you may be able to bear it". 1 Corinthians 10:13 (NKJV)

The Lord gives us the opportunity to face temptation, yet not *'fall'* in and abandon ourselves to it. He allows it to encourage us to do the right thing,to prove us good and acceptable. The tests or trials of God therefore imply His approval, His confidence in us, not His condemnation.

The Lord can 'test' His children in terms of our: faith, obedience, love, giving, patience, faithfulness, humility, hospitality, doing good and so on – virtues that it is good to be developed in us. God never tests or tries His own with anything that leads to sin. We need to remember that at the end of every test or trial of God stands righteousness.

In the paragraph below headed 'The Lord tried the Israelites' we see that the Lord can 'give' the unfaithful and the ungodly 'over' to the sinfulness of their hearts. However, this is not the Lord tempting!

To guide your prayerful identification of whether you are facing temptation, test or trial, let us look first at Biblical examples of the nature of the tests or trials of God.

The Lord tested Abraham

Genesis 22:1-2 and Hebrews 11:17, 19

Depending on the version of the Bible you read, in Genesis 22:1-2 you may read that God 'tempted' Abraham (KJV) or that He 'tested' Abraham in most other versions. Given that, as we have just read in James 1:13, the Lord does not tempt, what are we to make of this? In these matters, I like to go back to the original Hebrew and the context in which a word was used. In Chapter 2, 'Temptation Defined', I explained that the word 'tempted' used in the Old Testament is *'nasah'*, that is to test', 'to try' and 'to prove' something. This is the same word used in the Genesis 22:1 in the King James Version. Hebrews 11: 17 and 19 further backs up the fact that God is 'trying' not 'tempting' Abraham, the same King James Version reads: "By faith Abraham, when he was tried, offered up Isaac: and he that had received the promises offered up his only begotten son."

In Genesis 22:1-2, therefore the Lord 'tried' Abraham to 'prove' his faith and obedience. And when Abraham had passed the test, the Lord swore an oath, by His name, to bless Abraham and his seed.

This is a classic example of how the Lord 'proves to approve' rather than 'tests to condemn'.

The Lord tried the Israelites

Deuteronomy 8:2

In Deuteronomy 8:2, we read that God allowed the Israelites to wander in the wilderness for forty years. In fact, He was 'trying' their faithfulness.

When they forgot His miraculous deliverance from Egypt, gave into their cravings, sinned against Him, in unfaithfulness made and worshipped idols, strange gods, Psalm 81:12 says the Lord said:

"I am the LORD your God who brought you up out of Egypt. Open wide your mouth and I will fill it. "But my people would not listen to me; Israel would not submit to me. So I gave them over to their stubborn hearts to follow their own devices."

Through their years of wandering, the Lord did not Himself entice them to sin. He in fact, whenever they sinned, once they repented, He brought His people through the adversity and affliction they brought upon themselves.

The Lord tested the woman at Zarephath

1 Kings 17:8-16

In 1 Kings 17:8-16 we see the case of the Prophet Elijah and the woman at Zarephath:

"Then the word of the LORD came to him: "Go at once to Zarephath of Sidon and stay there. I have commanded a widow in that place to supply you with food." So he went to Zarephath. When he came to the town gate, a widow was there gathering sticks. He called to her and asked, "Would you bring me a little water in a jar so I may have a drink?" As she was going to get it, he called, "And bring me, please, a piece of bread." "As surely as the LORD your God lives," she replied, "I don't have any bread – only a handful of flour in a jar and a little oil in a jug. I am gathering a few sticks to take home and make a meal for myself and my son, that we may eat it – and die." Elijah said to her, "Don't be afraid. Go home and do as you have said. But first make a small cake of bread for me from what you have and bring it to me, and then make something for yourself and your son. For this is what the LORD, the God of Israel, says: 'The jar of flour will not be used up and the jug of oil will not run dry until the day the LORD gives rain on the land.'" She went away and did as Elijah had told her. So there was food every day for Elijah and for the woman and her family. For the jar of flour was not used up and the jug of oil did not run dry, in keeping with the word of the LORD spoken by Elijah."

Even though the words 'test' or 'trial' are not used in this particular story, I personally believe this was a clear test from God. The Lord was testing the woman in terms of her 'giving' and 'hospitality'. The Prophet, under God's instruction, demanded that the woman first 'give' to him. When the woman obeyed and gave to him out of the last that she had, God's divine intention to bless the woman was demonstrated. The Lord multiplied what she had. Verse 16 of 1 Kings 17 says:

"For the jar of flour was not used up and the jug of oil did not run dry, in keeping with the word of the LORD spoken by Elijah." This is how the Lord works. Though it is a bit of an aside, I want us to note something important here. Unlike this woman, just like Cain in Genesis 4:9-15, most people when giving to God, do not give out of their best, but rather of their surplus. When we do this, we have failed God's 'giving' test. There is a divine principle at work here. When you fail in the 'giving' test, it in turn affects what you receive; that is, God's provision in your life. God deserves the best; the first, the most valuable and the most precious of our substance (see Proverbs 3:9-10). When you obediently give to God, He also generously provides what you need; just as He did for the woman at Zarephath. 2 Corinthians 9:8 reads:

"Remember this: Whoever sows sparingly will also reap sparingly, and whoever sows generously will also reap generously. Each man should give what he has decided in his heart to give, not reluctantly or under compulsion, for God loves a cheerful giver. And God is able to make all grace abound to you, so that in all things at all times, having all that you need, you will abound in every good work."

Jesus tested the faith of the Canaanite woman

Matthew 15:21-28

"Leaving that place, Jesus withdrew to the region of Tyre and Sidon. A Canaanite woman from that vicinity came to him, crying out, "Lord, Son of David, have mercy on me! My daughter is suffering terribly from demon-possession." Jesus did not answer a word. So his disciples came to him and urged him, "Send her away, for she keeps crying out after us." He answered, "I was sent only to the lost sheep of Israel." The woman came and knelt before him. "Lord, help me!" she said. He replied, "It is not right to take the children's bread and toss it to their dogs." "Yes, Lord," she said, "but even the dogs eat the crumbs that fall from their masters' table." Then Jesus answered, "Woman, you have great faith! Your request is granted." And her daughter was healed from that very hour."

This woman had so much faith in Jesus that she would not allow anything she knew or heard; not even from Jesus Himself, to discourage her. In her humility, the Canaanite woman resisted the temptation to give a negative response to Jesus, or indeed give up hope. Instead, she focused on her faith in Jesus' healing power and probably her knowledge of Him (she called Him, 'Lord' and identified Him as 'Master'!). As a result, her request was granted and her daughter healed. Would we have had the presence of mind to resist the temptation to retaliate in response to what could be interpreted as an insult? Think about it!

The Temptation of Job

Job 1:8-12, KJV

"Then the LORD said to Satan, "Have you considered my servant Job? There is no one on earth like him; he is blameless and upright, a man who fears God and shuns evil." "Does Job fear God for nothing?" Satan replied. "Have you not put a hedge around him and his household and everything he has? You have blessed the work of his hands, so that his flocks and herds are spread throughout the land. But stretch out your hand and strike everything he has, and he will surely curse you to your face." The LORD said to Satan, "Very well, then, everything he has is in your hands, but on the man himself do not lay a finger." Then Satan went out from the presence of the LORD."

When we read about Job's situation, it begs the question why did God allow Satan to tempt His child, Job. We know now that God can and does allow of His children to be tempted. Just as with Job He allows it to "prove" us, worthy of His trust and able to stand and have victory over the temptation.

At the end of a gruelling set of tests we read in the Book of Job, eventually he recovered all and more!

Job received the 'promise of perseverance' at the end of his trials; he was blessed! There is a promise in perseverance.

James 1:12 says:

"Blessed is the man who perseveres under trial, because when he has stood the test, he will receive the crown of life that God has promised to those who love him." We have seen the evidence. The Lord promised to bless Abraham. The Lord provided a sacrificial lamb and in the end, He did indeed bless Abraham and his seed. Despite their regular unfaithfulness, when they repented, the Lord blessed His people, Israel. He sustained the little oil and flour of the woman of Zarepheth; she never ran out. He healed the Canaanite woman's daughter and He restored Job! In his tests, God refines us like gold through a process designed to bring out the best in us, not to destroy us.

Enduring God's tests or trials can be likened to a woman in labour. During childbirth, the woman goes through serious pain and discomfort. However, I'm told, once the child is born she forgets the long period of gestation and the pain of childbirth and enjoys her new baby.

Enduring tests or trials from God can also be likened to academic examinations. Students often find exams gruelling and painful, but they are an exercise undertaken for their own good, to approve their ability or standard. Students who go through examination successfully acquire certificates that give them better jobs and a better standard of living.

***

The Temptations of the Devil

We have seen that in his efforts to tempt, the Devil's purpose is to cause us to disobey God and sin against Him. We have observed that he desires for us to fall from our position of favour, beauty, riches, and health; our position of Grace.

It is the role he has played from the beginning of man's existence in the Garden of Eden. Satan has always tried to tempt man from the love of God, with the love of the world (that is, the lust of the flesh, the lust of the eye, and the pride of life). In Genesis 3:6 we read:

"When the woman saw that the fruit of the tree was good for food and pleasing to the eye, and also desirable for gaining wisdom, she took some and ate it. She also gave some to her husband, who was with her, and he ate it."

Eve, *saw* that 'the fruit of the tree of the knowledge of good and evil' (Genesis 2:17) was "good for food" – and desired to eat it, this is the 'lust of the flesh'.

She *observed* that it was "pleasing to the eye" – 'lust of the eyes'; and that it was and *realised* that it was "desirable for gaining wisdom" – the pride of life.

Let us look at four of the many flawed characteristics of mankind that can be the source of our temptation or be used by Satan to get a foothold in our lives.

Our Weaknesses

One of the Devil's major weapons is to tempt us in the area of our weakness. We need to be aware and identify our personal areas of weakness; and recognise when we are being tempted in them.

Job 3:25 illustrates that Job was tempted in his area of weakness, when Job says:

"What I feared has come upon me, and what I dreaded has happened to me."

Clearly, Job's weakness was fear about something bad happening – it is a weakness that is as common today as it has ever been. Like us, Job worried that something bad could happen to his family. In Job 1:5 we read about Job's ritual purification of his children:

"When a period of feasting had run its course, Job would send and have them purified. Early in the morning, he would sacrifice a burnt offering for each of them, thinking, "Perhaps my children have sinned and cursed God in their hearts."

Satan used Job's worst fear against him. Despite Job's post-feast purifications, all ten of Job's children (seven sons and three daughters) were killed when one of the brother's houses they were in, collapsed on top of them (Job 1:18-19). Cruelly, they were killed during one of their feasts! I imagine this would have intensified Job's agony – not having had the opportunity to purify his children against possible sin in his usual way (after a feast), before their deaths!

Our Evil Desires

We see this in James 1:14:

"... each one is tempted when, by his own evil desire, he is dragged away and enticed. For all bad and evil things comes from the devil"

As was in the beginning of man's existence, Satan is still enticing people with lusts of the flesh and of the eyes and the pleasures of selfish gain. He has a whole arsenal of evil desires at his disposal including: sexual immorality; impure thoughts; hostility; quarrelling; jealousy; anger; selfish ambition; divisions; conceit; envy; idolatry; demonic activities; drunkenness or alcoholism; drugs (Galatians 5:19-21); murder (Revelations 22:12-16); cheating (1 Corinthians 6:8); adultery; homosexuality; greed and stealing (1 Corinthians 6:9-10 and Ephesians 5:5); as well as lying (Revelations 22:12-16).

Given the deadly consequences, we must make every effort to actively resist and desist from these things. For not only are they sins against God in themselves, their practice ruins lives, brings shame, disgrace, sickness, and ultimately death.

Our Doubt

'Doubt', a lack of confidence and uncertainty in God's Word, is one of the greatest weapons Satan uses against the children of God. Like Eve, if the devil can manipulate you into doubting and consequently disobeying God, he has succeeded in causing you to sin against the Lord. When you separate yourself from Him; and waiver in your faith, this has deadly consequences. We can be robbed of the blessings of God and face lack and instability. James 1:5-8 says:

"If any of you lacks wisdom, let him ask of God, who gives to all liberally and without reproach, and it will be given to him. But let him ask in faith, with no doubting, for he who doubts is like a wave of the sea driven and tossed by the wind. For let not that man suppose that he will receive anything from the Lord; he is a double-minded man, unstable in all his ways." NKJV

Let us look at a few examples of the incidence and consequences of doubt in the Bible.

The King's Officer who doubted the word of the Prophet faced the consequences of doubt. In 2 Kings 7:1-2 we read:

"Then Elisha said, "Hear the word of the Lord. Thus says the Lord: 'Tomorrow about this time a seah of fine flour shall be sold for a shekel, and two seahs of barley for a shekel, at the gate of Samaria.' So an officer on whose hand the king leaned answered the man of God and said, "Look, if the Lord would make windows in heaven, could this thing be?" And he said, "In fact, you shall see it with your eyes, but you shall not eat of it." KJV.

Consequently, in 2 Kings 7:17, we read:

"Now the king had appointed the officer on whose hand he leaned to have charge of the gate. But the people trampled him in the gate, and he died, just as the man of God had said, who spoke when the king came down to him." 2 Kings 7:1-2, 17, NKJV

Zachariah was struck dumb until his son was born, because he doubted the Word of the Angel of the Lord.

"Zachariah asked the angel, "How can I be sure of this? I am an old man and my wife is well along in years." The angel answered, "I am Gabriel. I stand in the presence of God, and I have been sent to speak to you and to tell you this good news. And now you will be silent and not able to speak until the day this happens, because you did not believe my words, which will come true at their proper time." Luke 1:18-20

Jesus did not perform many miracles in His own hometown because His own people doubted him.

"Now it came to pass, when Jesus had finished these parables that He departed from there. And when He had come to His own country, He taught them in their synagogue, so that they were astonished and said, "Where did this Man get this wisdom and these mighty works? Is this not the carpenter's son? Is not His mother called Mary? And His brothers James, Joses, Simon, and Judas? And His sisters, are they not all with us? Where then did this Man get all these things?" So they were offended at Him. But Jesus said to them, "A prophet is not without honour except in his own country and in his own house." Now He did not do many mighty works there because of their unbelief." Matthew 13:53-58, NKJV

We need to be careful of anything or anybody that entices us to disobey God or to doubt His Word. Deuteronomy 13:6 says:

"If your very own brother, or your son or daughter, or the wife you love, or your closest friend secretly entices you, saying, "Let us go and worship other gods" (gods that neither you nor your fathers have known, gods of the peoples around you, whether near or far, from one end of the land to the other), do not yield to him or listen to him."

Remember whenever we are being enticed to doubt or disobey God; we are being drawn away to separate us from God and His blessings.

Our Disobedience

'Disobedience' a refusal or failure to obey, for a believer it is doing things in our own way instead of God's way. As it is a serious sin in the sight of God and breaks our fellowship with Him; it is one of Satan's primary areas of manipulation.

We will see in the next chapter 'How to be Successful in Temptation, Test or Trial' that with Adam and Eve, disobedience had such serious consequences; that it led to the fall of mankind as a whole.

Here are three Biblical examples of disobedience in action and their consequences.

Sadly, after all his years of toil, Moses was not allowed to enter the Promised Land because of his disobedience. If you read the whole of Numbers 20:1-12 you find that Moses disobeyed the instructions of the Lord to 'speak to that rock before their eyes' (Numbers 20:8). Instead, in his frustration with the people, Moses struck it twice. Numbers 20:12 says:

"Then the Lord spoke to Moses and Aaron, "Because you did not believe Me, to hallow Me in the eyes of the children of Israel, therefore you shall not bring this assembly into the land which I have given them." NKJV

In 1 Samuel 13:11-14, Saul lost his kingship due to his disobedience.

And Samuel said, "What have you done?" And Saul said, "When I saw that the people were scattered from me, and that you did not come within the days appointed, and that the Philistines gathered together at Michmash, then I said, 'The Philistines will now come down on me at Gilgal, and I have not made supplication to the Lord.' Therefore I felt compelled, and offered a burnt offering." And Samuel said to Saul, "You have done foolishly. You have not kept the commandment of the Lord your God, which He commanded you. For now the Lord would have established your kingdom over Israel forever but now your kingdom shall not continue. The Lord has sought for Himself a man after His own heart, and the Lord has commanded him to be commander over His people, because you have not kept what the Lord commanded you." NKJV

Paul warned the church at Ephesus not to give in to contradictory advice that leads to disobedience to God's Word, which results in the wrath of God. He said, "Let no one deceive you with empty words, for because of these things the wrath of God comes upon the sons of disobedience." Ephesians 5:6, NKJV

Paul also warned the Thessalonians in 2 Thessalonians 1:8-9: "He will punish those who do not know God and do not obey the gospel of our Lord Jesus. They will be punished with everlasting destruction and shut out from the presence of the Lord and from the majesty of his power."

Our weaknesses, evil desires, doubts and our disobedience are obvious frailties that Satan can use. There are many others, and these are just examples. Though Satan may use our frailties it is we who sin and we bear the responsibility.

Nevertheless, as I've said earlier, Satan's devices are not always obvious. The temptation to sin can be presented in other ways.

Even how others receive our kindness, for example, can be used by Satan as an opportunity to tempt us to sin. When we are asked to do good or help someone; or are doing good of our own accord (particularly someone we have regard for, even a fellow Christian) and the person we've helped doesn't show appreciation – our hurt or indignation can become a foothold for Satan. Which is why Galatians 6:9 advises us:

"Let us not be weary in well doing: for in due season we shall reap, if we faint not"

In this case and all other cases of temptation, test and trial, the devil's purpose is to challenge God and rob us of God's blessings.

***

How To Be Successful In Temptation, Test And Trial

It takes maturity in Christ and being prepared to be able to resist enticements to sin, and stand firm in faith.

We have to have a deep and committed relationship with the Lord. We must walk with Him, and seek to be in His presence continually. We need to know Him for ourselves, being rooted, and grounded in the Word of God. We cannot be like those referred to in Luke 8:11-13 who hear the word and believe for a while: "but in the time of testing they fall away"

When we draw near and put our trust in Him during temptation, test or trial, we will see the awesome power of our Lord in action. He will prove to us that we can rely totally on His wisdom and strength to bring us through. 2 Peter 2:9 says: "the Lord knows how to rescue godly men from trials and to hold the unrighteous for the day of judgement." Many times out of ignorance and immaturity we tend to think God has abandoned us when our expectations are delayed not realising that "delays are not denial".

If we are not spiritually mature, we may not be able to endure the temptations we face. In terms of the trial and tests of the Lord, we already know that as believers our loving and merciful Lord will never give us more than we can carry. I remember years ago because I was young in the Lord I was moaning about a situation I was going through and a friend quoted 1 Corinthians 10:13 saying the Lord knows that you are able to bear that is why He has allow you to go through that. Hearing and reading the quotation, I became settled and felt at peace. Paul said: No temptation has overtaken you except such as is common to man; but God *is* faithful, who will not allow you to be tempted beyond what you are able, but with the temptation will also make the way of escape, that you may be able to bear *it*. (NKJV)

As every scripture is inspired by God and is "useful for teaching, rebuking, correcting and training in righteousness" (2 Timothy 3:16), to guide us in taking a stand against temptation, and persevering through trials; I've looked at the approach to withstand temptation, adopted by a selection of the people in the Bible (some of whose experiences we've already touched upon). I have highlighted here two unsuccessful and four successful approaches to temptation, test and trial, which I call 'The Methods'.

1. The Adam & Eve Method
2. The David Method
3. The Abraham Method
4. The Job Method
5. The Joseph Method, and
6. The Jesus Method

With each approach, I have cited the critical lesson we should learn from it, and its key scriptural references.

Let us first look at the two unsuccessful approaches to withstand temptation I want to focus on; the classic, original unsuccessful approaches, 'The Adam & Eve Method' and then 'The David's Method'.

The Adam & Eve Method

Critical lesson: 'Do not Doubt' and 'Never Disobey'

Key Scripture: Genesis 3:1-7

We know Adam and Eve were tempted by the devil; he succeeded in causing them to doubt and disobey God. Because of their sin they 'fell', from grace dragging us all into sin with them!

"Now the serpent was more crafty than any of the wild animals the LORD God had made. He said to the woman, "Did God really say, 'You must not eat from any tree in the garden'?" The woman said to the serpent, "We may eat fruit from the trees in the garden, but God did say, 'You must not eat fruit from the tree that is in the middle of the garden, and you must not touch it, or you will die.'" "You will not surely die," the serpent said to the woman. "For God knows that when you eat of it your eyes will be opened, and you will be like God, knowing good and evil." When the woman saw that the fruit of the tree was good for food and pleasing to the eye, and also desirable for gaining wisdom, she took some and ate it. She also gave some to her husband, who was with her, and he ate it. Then the eyes of both of them were opened, and they realized they were naked; so they sewed fig leaves together and made coverings for themselves."

God had already said in Genesis 2:16-17:

"And the Lord God commanded the man, "You are free to eat from any tree in the garden; but you must not eat from the tree of the knowledge of good and evil, for when you eat of it you will surely die."

But Satan succeeded in tempting Eve to sin through doubt and disobedience (Genesis 2:4-6). Satan tempted Eve to go against the will of God, which brought death (separation from God), into the world and finally the fall of man.

Take note, if doubt and disobedience damaged the relationship between Adam and Eve and the Lord, it will do the same to you. No matter who you are, how long you have been in Church, or what position you hold; doubting God's word as Eve did will rob you of your blessings. We thank God for His redemptive promise and its fulfilment through the seed of the woman – our Lord Jesus Christ – who has redeemed man and restored the relationship between us and God.

In spite of the salvation that comes through Jesus Christ our Lord, I want you to take lesson from Adam and Eve's method to confront the Devil's temptation that the result brought death to all humanity. The Devil is still going round through circumstances creating the feeling of confusion or uncertainty about what God has said in His word. This means that Devil is causing people to suspect that God is not sincere or trustworthy, or that He is not true, likely, or genuine, a great sin that can cause anybody to be separated from the grace of God.

Most importantly, I want you to note as Jesus said as recorded by His brother James, whenever you are tempted by the Devil to doubt God in any circumstance notice that he is trying to deny you from receiving the best from God. Matt 21:21 says " So Jesus answered and said to them, "Assuredly, I say to you, if you have faith and do not doubt, you will not only do what was done to the fig tree, but also if you say to this mountain, 'Be removed and be cast into the sea,' it will be done". (NKJV)

But let him ask in faith, with no doubting, for he who doubts is like a wave of the sea driven and tossed by the wind. For let not that man suppose that he will receive anything from the Lord; *he is* a double-minded man, unstable in all his ways. James 1:6-8 (NKJV)

Never doubt God, no matter what, have faith in Him and everything will become possible with you

Like Adam and Eve your doubt can lead you to disobey God. As I said earlier, God had already said in Genesis 2:16-17:

"And the Lord God commanded the man, "You are free to eat from any tree in the garden; but you must not eat from the tree of the knowledge of good and evil, for when you eat of it you will surely die."

Eve obeyed Satan and disobeyed God by eating the forbidding fruit. If you face any temptation, make sure your approach is not in disobedience to what God has said in His word. In other words, you are not doing what the devil is telling you which is contrary to God's word or His instruction to you. Whenever you face any temptation you must first know that the Devil is behind whatever you are compelled to do which will bring great repercussion upon you if you fail.

Read 1 Samuel 13:13 about Saul's disobedience when he offered a sacrifice; and also when he spared

Agag and the spoils of the Amalekites in 1 Samuel 15: 28-30

The David Method

Critical Lesson: Resist evil desires

Key Scripture: 2 Samuel 11 & 12

'The David Method', based on David's response, is a stark example of another wrong approach to adopt in the face of temptation.

David, chosen by God Himself to be King, is considered one of the greatest heroes in Hebrew history; and he is described in the Bible as a man 'the Lord hath sought out of God's own heart" (1 Samuel 13:14, Acts 13:22).

David was a boy, a man and then a King prophetically blessed by God. He had a deep passion for God and His laws, a commitment, and a devotion to Him. Yet, David committed a number of monumental sins, when he failed to turn his back on temptation set before him by the Devil. This great and noble King who had the whole of the kingdom of Israel and Judah at his disposal *fell* headlong into temptation. The consequences of David's lack of self-control affected not just him and his children; but his family unto generations and the whole nation of Israel.

We pick up the account from 2 Samuel 11:1:
"In the spring, at the time when kings go off to war, David sent Joab out with the king's men and the whole Israelite army. They destroyed the Ammonites and besieged Rabbah. But David remained in Jerusalem."

Kind David, despite being the Commander of his army, stayed home when the entire Israelite army went to fight the Ammonites. By this time, he and his army had extended the borders of Israel, through military conquest and secured them against the surrounding nations. David's army had already defeated the Syrians hired by the Ammonites to fight on their behalf. David probably thought that defeating the Ammonites was a feat his men could achieve without him, so he took time-off, a rest from war.

It was during this period of 'rest', when David seemed to have time on his hands (he got up from bed in the evening, a classic symptom of sleeping during the day!) that his moment of temptation arrived. 2 Samuel 11:2 says:

"One evening David got up from his bed and walked around on the roof of the palace. From the roof he saw a woman bathing. The woman was very beautiful."

David 'saw a woman bathing, and the woman was very beautiful'. We hear echoes here of Eve in the Garden in Genesis 3:6, Eve:

"Saw that the fruit of the tree was good for food and pleasing to the eye"

Just as Eve had been, David was drawn away from the love of God, by the *lust of the eyes one of the Devil's channels of tempting.*

At this point, even though it is hard to do at times David could have averted his eyes; he could have come down from the roof and returned to his bed chamber so that he wouldn't have fallen into the temptation. He should have! This is the cry of everyone who, with hindsight looks back at the devastation their sin has caused "I should have not looked further" but is it is said 'had I known is always the last thing said'.

James 1:14-15 says "but each one is tempted when, by his own evil desire, he is dragged away and enticed. Then, after desire has conceived, it gives birth to sin; and sin, when it is full-grown, gives birth to death."

In not resisting temptation, in not running away from it, like Joseph did who we'll read about in 'The Joseph Method; in this Chapter, evil desire was conceived and sin born in David. David stayed on the roof and watched Bathsheba bathing!

David's evil desire? Through the lust of the eyes, he desired something that he should not have. What was his sin at this point? He had transgressed Levitical laws. He had looked on the nakedness of a woman (Leviticus 18), and he was contemplating having sex with a woman who was not his wife. 2 Samuel 11:3 says:

"and David sent someone to find out about her. The man said, "Isn't this Bathsheba, the daughter of Eliam and the wife of Uriah the Hittite?" Then David sent messengers to get her. She came to him, and he slept with her. (She had purified herself from her uncleanness.) Then she went back home."

When he discovered who she was; the wife of one of his own men, and still sent messengers to go and 'get her' for him and slept with her, David sinned.

He ignored the commandments of his Lord, which he had delighted in throughout his life. Specifically, Exodus 20:17,

'You shall not covet your neighbour's wife'

To summarise what happened next. There were lasting consequences from David's fall. Bathsheba became pregnant from their adulterous liaison. Fearing discovery of his sin and shame David sent for Uriah, with the hope that Uriah would go home and sleep with Bathsheba. But, Uriah, in contrast to David, showed integrity:

"Uriah said to David, "The ark and Israel and Judah are staying in tents, and my master Joab and my lord's men are camped in the open fields. How could I go to my house to eat and drink and lie with my wife? As surely as you live, I will not do such a thing!"" 2 Samuel 11:11

David's next scheme was to convince Uriah to stay for a day so that he could try and get Uriah drunk. But, Uriah still didn't go home, 'he slept on a mat among his master's servants' (2 Samuel 11:14)

Growing impatient with the situation David writes a letter to Joab, which he gives to Uriah to deliver, and Uriah does so faithfully, not knowing that the letter sealed his own doom, his death warrant. David wrote:

""Put Uriah in the front line where the fighting is fiercest. Then withdraw from him so he will be struck down and die."" 2 Samuel 11:14

Uriah is consequently killed by the Ammonites, and after the standard period of mourning. David married Bathsheba. The Bible says:

"But the thing David had done displeased the LORD." 2 Samuel 11:25

Because of the Lord's displeasure, we see the lasting, generational consequences. Nathan the Prophet came to David and told him what the Lord was saying about the consequences of what he, had done:

""Why did you despise the word of the LORD by doing what is evil in his eyes? You struck down Uriah the Hittite with the sword and took his wife to be your own. You killed him with the sword of the Ammonites. Now, therefore, the sword will never depart from your house, because you despised me and took the wife of Uriah the Hittite to be your own.' "'This is what the LORD says: 'Out of your own household I am going to bring calamity upon you. Before your very eyes I will take your wives and give them to one who is close to you, and he will lie with your wives in broad daylight. You did it in secret, but I will do this thing in broad daylight before all Israel.'" Then David said to Nathan, "I have sinned against the LORD."

Nathan replied, "The LORD has taken away your sin. You are not going to die. But because by doing this you have made the enemies of the LORD show utter contempt, the son born to you will die.""
2 Samuel 2:9-14

Despite his earnest repentance, which prompts David to write Psalm 51, everything the Lord spoke of happened. The foundation he erected affected his generations very badly. The child born to David and Bathsheba dies (2 Samuel 12:15-18). Amnon, David's first-born son, raped his own half-sister Tamar (2 Samuel 13:28-29). Amnon is killed by her brother, his half-brother Absalom (2 Samuel 13:28-29). Absalom rebels against his father David and sleeps with 10 of his father's concubines (2 Samuel 16:20-23). Adonijah, David's fourth son was executed on the orders of his half-brother Solomon (1 Kings 2:13-25)

We are all vulnerable to what we see but the lesson I am trying to teach here is that you may not be able to stop your eyes from looking but you can resist yourself from doing anything further that is wrong, like David's further action after he saw Bathsheba's nakedness. To be tempted is not sin but your wrong actions after, like David's experience with Bathsheba is sin. Nevertheless, like David if you are reading this book and you find yourself in the devil's trap because you did not exercise self-control God is willing to forgive you of any iniquity you have committed just as he did for David.

Now, let us move to discuss far more successful approaches used by other people which we should adopt.

The Abraham Method

Critical Lesson: 'Know that God will provide'

Key Scripture: Genesis 22:7-8

God tested Abraham with an instruction to sacrifice his only son Isaac to Him. With his faith in God and obedience to His command, Abraham held fast to his conviction that 'God will provide'.

From a synopsis of the Abraham story in the book of Genesis, we know that God spoke to him when he was called Abram, making a covenant with him at the age of 75. In Chapter 15, Abram asked God how, since he was childless, his seed would inherit his estate when he died. Verse 5 tells us that the Lord asked Abram to come outside and count the stars. When he was unable to count them, the Lord said to him that his descendants would be as numerous as the stars

In Chapter 17, the Lord appeared to Abram and said, "I am God Almighty; serve me faithfully and live a blameless life." (NLT) And He changed his name from 'Abram' to 'Abraham'.

In Chapter 18, we read that the Angel of the Lord visited Abraham and said to him that by the same time next year he, the angel, would return and Abraham would have a child. God fulfilled His promise in Chapter 21 giving Abraham a son, whom Abraham named 'Isaac' meaning *laughter*.

Then, in Chapter 22 we read that God 'tested' Abraham, asking him to sacrifice this very same son, Isaac to Him: "Take your son, your only son – yes, Isaac, whom you love so much – and go to the land of Moriah. Sacrifice him there as a burnt offering on one of the mountains, which I will point out to you." The next morning Abraham got up early. He saddled his donkey and took two of his servants with him, along with his son Isaac. Then he chopped wood to build a fire for a burnt offering and set out for the place where God had told him to go." Genesis 22:1-3, NLT

In verses 7 and 8 of Chapter 22 we read: "Abraham!" God called. "Yes," he replied. "Here I am."

"On his way with his son to the place of the sacrifice Isaac said, "Father?" "Yes, my son," Abraham replied. "We have the wood and the fire," said the boy, "but where is the lamb for the sacrifice?" "God will provide a lamb, my son," Abraham answered. And they both went on together." NLT

We know that Abraham was very sure when he said to Isaac, 'God will provide', because Genesis 21:12 says:

"But God told Abraham, "Do not be upset over the boy and your servant wife. Do just as Sarah says, for

Isaac is the son through whom your descendants will be counted." NLT

Therefore, "It was by faith that Abraham offered Isaac as a sacrifice when God was testing him. Abraham, who had received God's promises, was ready to sacrifice his only son, Isaac, though God had promised him, "Isaac is the son through whom your descendants will be counted."" Hebrews 11:17, NLT

'God will provide' was Abraham's method and God did indeed provide.

"When they arrived at the place where God had told Abraham to go, he built an altar and placed the wood on it. Then he tied Isaac up and laid him on the altar over the wood. And Abraham took the knife and lifted it up to kill his son as a sacrifice to the Lord. At that moment, the angel of the Lord shouted to him from heaven, "Abraham! Abraham!" "Yes," he answered. "I'm listening." "Lay down the knife," the angel said. "Do not hurt the boy in any way, for now I know that you truly fear God. You have not withheld even your beloved son from me." Then Abraham looked up and saw a ram caught by its horns in a bush. So he took the ram and sacrificed it as a burnt offering on the altar in place of his son. Abraham named the place "The Lord Will Provide" (Jehovah Jireh). This name has now become a proverb: "On the mountain of the Lord it will be provided."'" Genesis 22:9-14, NLT

Abraham was fully persuaded, having total confidence that even if Isaac died, God who is the giver of life was able to bring Isaac back to life. In a sense, Abraham did receive his son back from the dead (see Hebrews 11:17-19).

In his letter to the Romans, this is what Paul has to say about Abraham's faith:

"That is what the Scriptures mean when God told him, "I have made you the father of many nations." This happened because Abraham believed in the God who brings the dead back to life and who creates new things out of nothing. Even when there was no reason for hope, Abraham kept hoping – believing that he would become the father of many nations. For God had said to him, "That's how many descendants you will have!" And Abraham's faith did not weaken, even though, at about 100 years of age, he figured his body was as good as dead – and so was Sarah's womb. Abraham never wavered in believing God's promise. In fact, his faith grew stronger, and in this, he brought glory to God. He was fully convinced that God is able to do whatever he promises. And because of Abraham's faith, God counted him as righteous."Romans 4:17-22, NLT

Even though Abraham was about 100 years old and his wife, Sarah was also old and past her childbearing years; Abraham believed that God was able to do what He had promised.

Abraham did not consider the natural evidence but believed the spiritual evidence the promises of God. Even though as a human being Abraham made some mistakes (one of his mistakes was when he listened to his wife's advice and had a son, Ishmael, with Hagar) he knew that God is always faithful to His promise. Therefore, he did not waver in his faith, but became stronger and stronger in it.

The account continues. After Abraham had used the provided ram for the sacrifice, the Lord again spoke to him, through The Angel of the Lord:

"Then the angel of the Lord called again to Abraham from heaven. "This is what the Lord says: Because you have obeyed me and have not withheld even your son, your only son, I swear by my own name that I will certainly bless you. I will multiply your descendants beyond number, like the stars in the sky and the sand on the seashore. Your descendants will conquer the cities of their enemies. And through your descendants all the nations of the earth will be blessed, all because you have obeyed me.""" Genesis 22:15-18. NLT

God did not really want Abraham to sacrifice Isaac He only tested his obedience. The only human sacrifice God ever required was the Lamb of God, Jesus Christ Himself. Amen!

As a father, consider for a moment the agony Abraham went through on the three days journey with his son. Remember this was his promised son, the one he loved! Can you imagine what thoughts were going through his head knowing that he would kill and burn his beloved son, at the request of God? Imagine the horror he must have felt within when Isaac asked him where the sacrificial lamb was. It could not have been easy, but one thing is certain, he was determined to obey God and he had serious faith. He knew that absolutely everything that he had, had been given to him by God, and so he in turn would withhold nothing from Him.

Like Abraham, many people are looking to God to provide unlike Abraham they are not following God's instructions; they are doing things in their own way! God provided because Abraham followed God's way. It is obvious from Abraham's experience that the provision of God works with obedience. If you obey, He provides. If you know you are being disobedient, it makes sense that you cannot then expect God to provide!

Abraham's Method is summed up in this equation:

Obedience + Faith = God will provide (God's provision)

Like Abraham, are you ready to obey, believe and make sacrifice to God? What is the most precious thing in your life? Are you prepared to give it to Him? It could be your life, your time, or your money? If you are prepared to obey, He will also provide. When the Lord, through His Word, asks you to do anything, no matter how hard and impossible it may seem to be, just believe, trust and obey. Know that the Lord is only testing you to bless you.

The Job Method

Critical Lesson: 'Do not sin by blaming' God.

Key Scripture Job 1:20-22

Job faced the bitterest of trials and tribulations, but in all Job did not sin by blaming God.

The truth of the matter, as we have noted earlier, was that God did indeed allow Satan to test Job. In Job Chapter 1, we see the Bible describe Job as a wealthy man of upright character, who loved God. Satan the 'accuser of the brethren' (Revelations 12:10) came before God claiming that Job was trusting God only because he, Job, was wealthy and everything was going well for him. It is interesting to note that the devil knows that it is the Lord that blesses!

"Then the Lord asked Satan, "Have you noticed my servant Job? He is the finest man in all the earth – a man of complete integrity. He fears God and will have nothing to do with evil." Satan replied to the Lord, "Yes, Job fears God, but not without good reason! You have always protected him and his home and his property from harm. You have made him prosperous in everything he does. Look how rich he is! But take away everything he has and he will surely curse you to your face!" "All right, you may test him," the Lord said to Satan. "Do whatever you want with everything he possesses, but don't harm him physically." So Satan left the Lord's presence." Job 1: 8-12, NLT.

Satan then decides to intensify his attack, we read in Job 2:4-6:

"Satan replied to the Lord, "Skin for skin, he blesses you only because you bless him. A man will give up everything he has to save his life. But take away his health, and he will surely curse you to your face!" "All right, do with him as you please," the Lord, said to Satan. "But spare his life."" NLT

Job then faced a series of catastrophic attacks against his faith, from Satan. First, we read in Job 1 verses 13-19 that Satan attacked Job's possessions.

In verses 13-15, Job received news that raiders had carried away his oxen and donkeys and all his labourers killed – except the one who carried the news. In verse 16, Job receives news that the fire of God came from the sky and destroyed all his sheep and his servants – all except the one who brought the news! In verse 17, Job receives news that the Chaldeans had formed three parties, swept down on his camels, carried them off and killed the servants – all except the one who brought the news. In verses 18 and 19, Job received the hardest news of all: the news that as they feasted in the older son's house, the building had collapsed killing all his sons and daughters.

This was the very thing Job feared and was trying to avoid by ritually purifying his children after feasts. His fear had come upon him! Job 3:25 "What I always feared has happened to me. What I dreaded has come true."

It is in verses 20-22 that we read:

"Job stood up and tore his robe in grief. Then he shaved his head and fell to the ground to worship. He said, "I came naked from my mother's womb, and I will be naked when I leave. The Lord gave me what I had, and the Lord has taken it away. Praise the name of the Lord!" In all of this, Job did not sin by blaming God." NLT.

Because of Job's reaction to overwhelming temptation, (the temptation of turning on God when situations get too difficult to handle) this was to be the beginning of what was to happen to Job. I believe that because, even in his darkest hour of pain and grief, Job 'fell to the ground to worship' and he praised the name of the Lord, Satan persisted. Satan's second series of attacks were attacks on Job's very body and person.

In Job chapter 2 after Job had withstood the first test, when he did not give up, sin or blame God – Satan went to God a second time, and again God permitted him to test Job further. In Job 2:1-7, God allowed Job's health to be taken away, but not his life.

On top of the loss of all his possessions including his children, then from verse 9 we read about the severe bouts of sickness Job experienced. Job's wife, of all people, who was supposed to stand by him, gave up on him. She advised him to curse God and die. Again, Job refused to sin against God and said to his wife in Job 2:10 "You are talking like a foolish woman. Shall we accept good from God, and not trouble?" NLT Job had no help from his wife.

In Job 2:8 his skins condition was so unbearable that he scraped his head with a piece of broken pottery. He looked so awful that even his own friends, who should have been able to, could not recognise him from a distance. There is an Akan proverb; loosely translated this means 'we don't need light in the darkness to be able to recognise someone we know very well'. Akan is a language group spoken by peoples mainly in Ghana and Côte d'Ivoire.

In Job 2:11-13 we read that his friends then sat down with him for seven days and nights, and no one spoke; because they saw that his suffering was too great for words. In his agony Job curses the day he was born, even stating in Job 3:1-19, that he wished he had been still born. Yet, the Bible says in all this, despite all of his suffering, Job continued to trust God.

In Job 3:1-31:40 we see Job's last mortal hope, his three friends, also give up on him. Eliphaz, Bildad and Zophar wrongly assumed that, suffering always comes as a result of sin so, Job must have sinned. They believed in the world of cause and effect, and with this in mind, they tried to persuade Job to repent (Job 5:8).

From Job chapter 32 to chapter 34, we read of a young man named Elihu, who, having listened to the entire conversation between Job and his friends, criticised them for not giving Job a satisfactory analysis of his situation. Nevertheless, unfortunately in Job chapters 35 and 36, in the end, he also got it wrong.

He said although Job was a good man, he had allowed himself to become proud, and God was punishing him in order to humble him. Like Elihu, there are many people today, who judge people that are going through temptation as being afflicted; because of their pride or lack of humility, which is so often not the case.

In Job 19:25-26 in response to his friend Bildad, Job said:

"But as for me, I know that my redeemer lives, and that he will stand upon the earth at last. And after my body has decayed, yet in my flesh I will see God or without my body I will see God." NLT

He did not give up his faith in God, he did not blame God, he said:

"Though He slay me, yet will I trust Him." Job 13:15, NKJV

This is awesome faith in adversity! As a result, God Himself answered in Job 38:1-41:34. The

Lord did not answer the series of questions Job was asking Him directly. Instead, God posed a series of questions nobody could answer. And in His response, Job recognised that God's ways are the best. Like Job, we must also come to know that God's time and ways are always the best and always humble ourselves before Him.

After many chapters describing Job's trials and tribulations, in Job 42:1-17 we read that Job was restored. A closer look at the reasons behind Job's temptation, trials and tribulations, confirms my point that God's intention in testing his children is to 'prove' them good and acceptable; and Satan's is the direct opposite.

Often when problems come, we give up so quickly, sin against God or curse God in the process. We do have a choice! We can learn so much from the story of Job about how to stand in faith in God. Job's experience enables us to understand that those who love God are not exempt from trouble. The Psalmist says, "Many are the afflictions of a righteous but the Lord delivers him from them all." Psalm 34:19, NKJV

When, through no fault of our own, we experience severe suffering, we should avoid adding to our pain by feeling guilty; questioning whether some hidden sin is causing our troubles. Suffering is a part of life. It is certainly to be experienced in our walk as followers of Jesus Christ. Matthew 10:22-25 says:

"All men will hate you because of me, but he who stands firm to the end will be saved. When you are persecuted in one place, flee to another. I tell you the truth, you will not finish going through the cities of Israel before the Son of Man comes. "A student is not above his teacher, nor a servant above his master. It is enough for the student to be like his teacher, and the servant like his master. If the head of the house has been called Beelzebub, how much more the members of his household!"

In temptation, we can take heart from the comforting fact that as demonstrated in the case of Job, Satan's power is limited. He cannot tempt us above what he has been permitted, by God. The Lord never allows more than we can carry. Satan twice had to ask God for permission to tempt Job, and that permission was conditional! The Lord said to Satan:

"Very well, then, everything he has is in your hands, but on the man himself do not lay a finger" Job 1:12 and "Very well, then, he is in your hands, but you must spare his life" Job 2:6

An important fact to note from Job's experience is that in times of temptation, test or trial we can lose something dear to us; Job lost all his wealth, including his children. To add to his woes, when he needed his wife's support the most, she disappointed him. Clearly, she had had enough! It goes without saying that, unlike Job's wife we must be supportive to our spouses in their times of temptation.

The message here is in times of temptation or trial, even if you lose something dear to you, and those you are counting on for support disappoint you, never give up. It is part of what you are facing; if you do not give in you will be restored. We must emulate Job and trust God that even if everything is taken away from us, we still have Him. He will never leave us nor forsake us. Isaiah 49:15 says:

"Can a mother forget the baby at her breast and have no compassion on the child she has borne? Though she may forget, I will not forget you!"

Know that if every hope and everybody deserts you, God will be with you.

It is important to realise that unlike Job's friends, when we see our friends suffering we need to support them and not accuse them. One of the problems with believers is that instead of interceding for our Christian brothers and sisters, who are caught up in 'trouble'; we tend to judge them and even ostracise them. We must be careful not to judge others who are suffering. We must be cautious maintaining the certainty of our knowledge of the Grace of God. His Grace is sufficient for all! (2 Corinthians 12:9). I will be looking at the significance of this aspect; dealing with temptation and judging others being tempted, in the concluding chapter of this guide.

From Job's questioning of God, we learn another important lesson. We should not demand that God explain everything, for not all the details of His plans are to be revealed to us:

"There are secret things that belong to the Lord our God, but the revealed things belong to us and our descendants forever, so that we may obey these words of the law." Deuteronomy 29:29, NLT

Job did not know why what was happening to him, was happening. He had not been party to the conversation between the Lord and Satan! Nevertheless, he still did not give up on God. We must do the same. Trust God even when we do not understand the problems or temptations we may face. In every temptation, test or trial that you find yourself in, it is important not to sin by saying anything against God. Never blame God! The Bible tells us that in everything we are to give Him thanks (Ephesians 5:20, Philippians 4:6 & 1 Thessalonians 5:18), "for all things works together for good to those who love God, to those who are the called according to his purpose" Romans 8:28, NKJ

Many of us could not go through an ordeal like the one Job did without complaining, bitterly. At the point when it looked like it was all over for him and hope was finished, Job kept silent. I personally believe that this was one reasons he was successful in his temptation, why he did not sin against God. In Job 27:2-6 though he was in serious pain, he vowed not to speak against God and maintained his integrity:

"As surely as God lives, who has denied me justice, the Almighty, who has made me taste bitterness of soul, as long as I have life within me, the breath of God in my nostrils, my lips will not speak wickedness, and my tongue will utter no deceit. I will never admit you are in the right; till I die, I will not deny my integrity. I will maintain my righteousness and never let go of it; my conscience will not reproach me as long as I live."

When we talk too much and complain about our trials we can worsen our situations by expressing doubt and possibly sinning against God, through the words we speak. When we tell the wrong people, what we are going through they can, and often do, turn our pain into gossip! When we get engrossed in conversation, we lose concentration; we do not apply faith to the situation and spend less time listening to God. In addition, in talking to others about our problems, we sometimes open ourselves up to negative and ungodly feedback. Therefore, in temptation, test and trial, we must guard our mouths! Someone once said *"don't talk about your problem, talk to it."*

The Joseph Method

Critical Lesson: 'Run from sin'

Key Scripture: Genesis 39:7-13

"And it came to pass after these things that his master's wife cast longing eyes on Joseph, and she said, "Lie with me." But he refused and said to his master's wife, "look, my master does not know what is with me in the house, and he has committed all that he has to my hand. "There is no one greater in this house than I, nor has he kept back anything from me but you, because you are his wife. How can I do this great wickedness, and sin against God?" So it was, as she spoke to Joseph day by day, that he did not heed her, to lie with her or to be with her. But it happened about this time, went into the house to do his work, and none of the men of the house was inside, that she caught him by the garment, saying, "Lie with me." But he left his garment in her hand, and fled and run outside." Genesis 39:7-13, NLT

When we look into the background of Joseph, we can understand why he handled this particular temptation in the way he did. Joseph was the last but one of Jacob and Rachel's children, and Jacob's favourite son (Genesis 30:22-25; 37:3). Joseph shared his God-given vision prematurely with his brothers, which resulted in them hating him (perhaps he said too much!). They threw him into a pit and sold him to Midianite traders (Genesis 37:25-28), who in turn sold him to Potiphar – an officer of Pharaoh, Captain of the Guard in Egypt (Genesis 39:1).

This is where Potiphar's wife comes in. When it seemed as though his dream was being fulfilled in his master's house, disaster struck again. Joseph was thrown into prison for refusing to sleep with Potiphar's wife – instead he ran from sin.

Yet, it still was not over for Joseph. Even in prison, the favour of God was upon him; he interpreted a fellow prisoners dreams (Genesis 40); but was then forgotten by those he helped (Genesis 41:8-13). Yet, Joseph still did not give up. He held onto God, and the Lord held on to him! – The Lord was with him.

Though it was not easy eventually the promise of God in Joseph's life, came to pass. He was finally called to interpret the dream of Pharaoh, because of his revelatory interpretation he became a Prime Minister (Genesis 41:37-44).

Here are the lessons we can learn from the Joseph story.

I believe that what matters are not so much the events or circumstances of our lives, but our response to them. Joseph, throughout his ordeals, *did not complain*. I believe he had his eyes on the vision, the promise he had received from God.

To be successful in temptation, first we need to have grasped what God has planned for us; His vision or promise for our lives. When we know, who we are and what we are called to do, we have a weapon to help us holdfast in the face of temptation. In waiting for the fulfilment of the promise, we can, as Joseph did, face troubles and trials. Like Joseph if we stay calm and never complain, we see the fulfilment of our dreams, our destiny.

The only way to deal with some temptations is to do like Joseph, especially the temptation of sexual immorality, run! Joseph was at a crucial point in his life. He was the most trusted officer in the house of Potiphar; he could practically do anything he wanted. It would seem from his reaction that

Joseph realised that Potiphar's wife's advances were a temptation from the devil (Genesis 39:9-12), had he succumbed to her advances, he would have committed a grave sin, and missed his destiny. Instead, he kept his eye, his focus on God. With God's help, any situation can be used for good, even when others intend evil.

Making this practical for our lives today, if someone invites you to his/her house and you suspect their intentions, or they have previously made sexual advances to you. For a start, do not go to their house alone. The wisest thing to do is to 'run' like Joseph; it is not the time to test your faith!

Have you ever been repaid evil for good; been forgotten by those you have helped? Have people you should have been able to count on deserted you? Then you know how painful it is. Joseph was punished for doing the right thing, imprisoned for many years and forgotten by those he helped.

Yet, in all these things the Bible says, God was with him and he eventually fulfilled the promise on his life. Do not worry if men, through unfaithfulness and their own selfishness, forget you and your good deeds – God is with and for you. I know it is hard, but remember that if you are repaid evil for good the Lord God, the righteous judge of all, will Himself compensate you. Galatians 6:9 says:

"Let us not become weary in doing good, for at the proper time we will reap a harvest if we do not give up."

I have already talked about it in 'The Job Method' but it is pertinent here too. In the face of your temptation, test or trial – do not complain. Complaining will take your eyes off God, set your attention on man and the circumstances; and eventually end in defeat. No matter what the enemy brings to you, hold on to your vision in faith. Whatever God has said concerning you will happen just as He said it would. Isaiah 55:10-11 says:

"As the rain and the snow come down from heaven, and do not return to it without watering the earth and making it bud and flourish, so that it yields seed for the sower and bread for the eater, so is my word that goes out from my mouth: It will not return to me empty, but will accomplish what I desire and achieve the purpose for which I sent it."

The Jesus Method

Critical Lesson: 'It Is Written ...' Use the Word

Key Scripture: Matthew 4:1-11

You will recall from 'The Adam & Eve Method' described at the beginning of this chapter, that Satan tempted Adam and Eve. They are not the only ones, he also tempted Christ, but, unlike Adam and Eve, Christ defeated the devil. Paul says in 1 Corinthians 15:45 the second Adam (Christ, the promised seed of the woman who would crush the head of the serpent) is wiser than the first Adam.

Our key scripture in Matthew 4: 1 – 11 says:

"Then Jesus was led by the Spirit into the desert to be tempted by the devil. After fasting forty days and forty nights, he was hungry. The tempter came to him and said, "If you are the Son of God, tell these stones to become bread."

Jesus answered, "It is written: 'Man does not live on bread alone, but on every word that comes from the mouth of God.'" Then the devil took him to the holy city and had him stand on the highest point of the temple. "If you are the Son of God," he said, "throw yourself down. For it is written: "'He will command his angels concerning you, and they will lift you up in their hands, so that you will not strike your foot against a stone.'" Jesus answered him, "It is also written: 'Do not put the Lord your God to the test.'" Again, the devil took him to a very high mountain and showed him all the kingdoms of the world and their splendour. "All this I will give you," he said, "if you will bow down and worship me." Jesus said to him, "Away from me, Satan! For it is written: 'Worship the Lord your God, and serve him only.'" Then the devil left him, and angels came and attended him."

The three areas of Jesus' temptation that we need to look at more closely, in order to learn valuable lessons, are temptations in the area of:

1. Physical need and desires
2. Power, and
3. Possession, Power and Pride

First temptation: Physical need and desires

"Then Jesus was led by the Spirit into the desert to be tempted by the devil. After fasting forty days and forty nights, he was hungry. The tempter came to him and said, "If you are the Son of God, tell these stones to become bread."-**Matthew 4:1-3**

Jesus' response:

"Jesus answered, "It is written: 'Man does not live on bread alone, but on every word that comes from the mouth of God.'"" **Matthew 4:4**

Jesus was referring to Deuteronomy 8:3 when the bible said:

"He humbled you, causing you to hunger and then feeding you with manna, which neither you nor your fathers had known, to teach you that man does not live on bread alone but on every word that comes from the mouth of the Lord."

The Devil who always tempts us with things we need or are vulnerable to, knew that Jesus – having fasted for forty days – was hungry, tired and lonely in the wilderness, so he tempted Him with the comfort of food. Jesus, though He needed sustenance also knew the time was not right for him to indulge himself, he knew he faced the enemy.

My dear reader I want you to know and consider this in your mind, the devil will not tempt you with anything you do not fancy or need. He will always come with something that will attract you, something you will find it difficult to say "No" to.

A practical application for this temptation in our lives is pre-marital sex. Although sex is a good thing attractive and appealing, it is not sinful in itself; but, it is wrong to have sex before and outside of marriage. There is a right time for everything.

Second Temptation: Power

"Then the devil took him to the holy city and had him stand on the highest point of the temple. "If you are the Son of God," he said, "throw yourself down. For it is written: 'He will command his angels concerning you, and they will lift you up in their hands, so that you will not strike your foot against a stone.'" **Matthew 4:5-6**

Jesus' response:

"Jesus answered him, "It is also written: 'Do not put the Lord your God to the test.'" **Matthew 4:7**

Jesus was referring to Deuteronomy 6:16, which says: "Do not test the Lord your God as you did at Massah."

Certainly, I believe it would have been easier for Jesus to 'throw' himself down, than it would have been for him to continue fasting whilst wandering in an inhospitable, dry desert! And indeed, angels would have lifted him, had he done so. Jesus knew Psalm 91:11-12 which says:

"For He will command His angels concerning you to guard you in all your ways; they will lift you up in their hands, so that you will not strike your foot against a stone."

However, the Lord also knew Satan's aim; to 'throw' himself down would have meant Jesus would be testing God. It would also have been the first time that the Lord Jesus Christ has obeyed Satan – something that never had and never could happen. Jesus obeying him would have result in Jesus' death because it would mean Him obeying the Devil and disobeying God.

Friends never underestimate the wickedness of the Devil. He is a wicked person that no one should tolerate. He said to Jesus "If you are the Son of God," Like the devil, men will trick you to move forward or do something in this context to throw yourself down when they know that there is danger or trouble ahead but the Lord will always keep his promise for you because of his faithfulness. Thank God, Jesus defeated him with his response "It is written" because Jesus knew his plans.

Once I watched a movie about a man who wanted to teach his son never to trust anyone. He taught a hard lesson; he took his son to a roof top and told him to stay there as he went down to teach him a lesson. Standing outside, he asked his son to jump down into his arms and he would catch him. In his innocence, the teenage boy jumped trusting that his father was going to catch him but he landed heavily on the ground. His father had moved out of the way at the last minute not making any attempt to catch him as he had promised. As he lay on the floor crying in pain as a result of injury he had sustained his father looked at him and said "Never trust any man, for man will disappoint you."

The man was right because I believe from that day the boy would never trust any man including his own father. The only person we can trust is God which is right thing to do. For unlike the devil God will never move out of the way or have any hidden agenda when He asks you to jump down for He is always faithful to his word waiting to catch you. Whatever He says He means it, it is real.

The Devil wanted to kill Jesus before his time through disobedience just as he did to Adam in the Garden of Eden but once again the Lord defeated him with the Word "It is also written: 'Do not put the Lord your God to the test.'" **Matthew 4:7** with the Word there is always going to be victory.

Third Temptation: Possession, Pride and Power

"Again, the devil took him to a very high mountain and showed him all the kingdoms of the world and their splendour. "All this I will give you," he said, "if you will bow down and worship me.'" **Matthew 4:8-9**

Jesus' response:

"Jesus said to him, "Away from me, Satan! For it is written: 'Worship the Lord your God, and serve him only.'" **Matthew 4:10**

Jesus exercised James 4:7 and quoted Deuteronomy 6:13.

In exercising James 4:7, He resisted the Devil, as we are warned to "… Resist the devil, and he will flee from you."

In quoting the Word written in Deuteronomy 6:13, He beat Satan with the weapon of the Word, which says, "Fear the LORD your God, serve him only and take your oaths in his name."

We can see from Jesus' temptation that temptation can come via a real need. Real needs can create appropriate and inappropriate desires that Satan can use to his advantage. The types of temptations the Lord Jesus Christ experienced are all very familiar to us today. We face the same kinds every day, but Jesus was victorious. He defeated the Devil because He did not give in to any of the Devil's enticements. With Jesus' temptation, I can re-enforce my view that to be tempted is not sin but to fall into temptation is sin

The primary lesson from 'The Jesus Method' then is that in the face of temptation use the Word. Jesus not only knew the Word of God, He also obeyed and applied it. It is not enough knowing the word; using or putting it into practice is also important. There are many believers today who are very good and can quote every scripture but do not apply it when the need be.

Jesus once teaching his disciples about The Wise and Foolish Builders story said "Therefore everyone who hears these words of mine and puts them into practice is like a wise man who built his house on the rock. The rain came down, the streams rose, and the winds blew and beat against that house;

yet it did not fall, because it had its foundation on the rock. But everyone who hears these words of mine and does not put them into practice is like a foolish man who built his house on sand. The rain came down, the streams rose, and the winds blew and beat against that house, and it fell with a great crash." Matt 7:21-27 (NIV)

James wrote to advice his readers when he said, "Do not merely listen to the word, and so deceive yourselves. Do what it says. Anyone who listens to the word but does not do what it says is like a man who looks at his face in a mirror and, after looking at himself, goes away and immediately forgets what he looks like. But the man who looks intently into the perfect law that gives freedom, and continues to do this, not forgetting what he has heard, but doing it—he will be blessed in what he does". James 1:21-25 (NIV)

Why is using the Word so important and Jesus' example so relevant? Hebrews 4:15 talks about Christ as our High Priest,

"This High Priest of ours understands our weakness, for he faced all the same temptations we do, yet he did not sin." NLT

Verse 16 says, "So let us come boldly to the throne of our gracious God. There we will receive his mercy, and we will find grace to help us when we need it." NLT

There is therefore no better example to follow, in our dealing with temptation than our own High Priest who faced, and defeated the very same temptations we face. Jesus demonstrates both the importance and the effectiveness of knowing and applying Scripture using "It is written" to combat temptation.

Without doubt, I know that the main problem for believers in following 'The Jesus Method' is that most of us do not know the Word. Most of us rarely use what is supposed to be the most effective offensive and defensive weapon for every believer. Ephesians 6:17 says:

"Take the helmet of salvation and the sword of the Spirit, which is the word of God."

Do you know what the Word says about your situation? Have you committed it to your heart? Can you reach for it and quote it as and when you need to in the face of temptation, as Jesus did? Do you have the "readiness that comes from the gospel of peace?" (Ephesians 6:15)? It is easy to fall into temptation and backslide if you do not know and obey the Word. In every form of temptation, test or trial you may be facing 'The Jesus Method' "It is written" offers the greatest solution to guarantee success.

Another important thing to note here is that the devil knows and misused the Word of God, even when quoting it to the Saviour Himself! The devil quoted Psalm 91:11-12, but did not obey it! If the devil knows and misuses the Word, I think we as believers really have a responsibility to know and apply the Word, which is appropriate to our situation and circumstances, ourselves. Otherwise the devil can and will use our own weapons against us.

Another comfort I want you to draw from Jesus' temptation is what the writer of the book of Hebrews wrote in Hebrews 2:18 (KJV) "For in that he himself hath suffered being tempted, he is able to succour them that are tempted." Never be discouraged and dismayed if you face any type of temptation for our High Priest, Jesus Christ who was tempted but defeated the devil is well able to deliver you, you are safe no matter what.

***

Joyful In Temptation

Apart from the many methods that helped many people including Jesus Christ to be successful in their temptation, test and trial, as we learnt earlier I have also identified yet another way that can help one to be successful. This is to be joyful, that is expressing great happiness when facing temptation, test or trial. What I mean is laughing in times of adversity, test and trials that come from God. When you express joy in times of difficulty, it gives you strength to face any challenge with a positive attitude that always produces victory. Thank God for Christianity, the only religion that teaches the followers through the Bible to be joyful in adversity knowing that the Lord is in control in any situation we face.

Ezra told the Israelites …Do not sorrow, for the joy of the Lord is your strength." Nehemiah 8:10 (NKJV) in other words joy is strength.

Expressing joy in any situation will always be followed by praise to God as demonstrated by Jesus Christ in Luke 10:21. At that time Jesus, full of joy through the Holy Spirit, said, "I praise you, Father, Lord of heaven and earth, because you have hidden these things from the wise and learned, and revealed them to little children. Yes, Father, for this is what you were pleased to do." (NIV)

The writer of the book of Hebrews entreats all believers to follow Jesus Christ, the example of our faith who endured the Cross because of the joy that was set before Him. He said, "Looking unto Jesus, the author and finisher of *our* faith, who for the joy that was set before Him endured the cross, despising the shame, and has sat down at the right hand of the throne of God" Hebrews 12:2 (NKJV). Jesus had the strength to go the cross because He faced it with joy. Do you need strength to deal with your temptation, test or trial? Be joyful.

Isaiah said, "Therefore with joy you will draw water, From the wells of salvation." Isaiah 12:3 (NKJV), this means that when you are joyful in any situation you will be reaching out for your rescue or deliverance.

Paul who himself with Silas prayed and sang praise to God in their dilemma that produced one of the greatest miracles recorded in the bible.

In Acts 16:25-26 "But at midnight Paul and Silas were praying and singing hymns to God, and the prisoners were listening to them. Suddenly there was a great earthquake, so that the foundations of the prison were shaken; and immediately all the doors were opened and everyone's chains were loosed." (NKJV) Knowing the power that is released when joy is expressed through prayer and praise in 1 Thessalonians 5:16-18 the great Apostle said, "Rejoice always, Pray without ceasing, In everything give thanks, for this is the will of God in Christ Jesus for you." (NKJV)

The above quotation commands believers to give thanks to the Lords at all times, as part of our praise to Him for this is the will of God in Christ Jesus for His children. As believers the end result of every temptation, test or trial will be for our good if we only know how to handle it. This means that nothing is by accident. All things are divinely approved, if we truly believe God is who we know he is "Jehovah" the great "I AM" the all-knowing God

For this reason Paul in Romans 5:1-4 (NKJV) says

"Therefore, having been justified by faith, we have peace with God through our Lord Jesus Christ, through whom also we have access by faith into this grace in which we stand, and rejoice in hope of the glory of God. *And not only that, but we also glory in tribulations,* **knowing** *that tribulation produces perseverance*; and perseverance, character; and character, hope."

Also in Romans 8:28 (NKJV) he said,

"And we know that all things work together for good to those who love God, to those who are the called according to His purpose."

Writing to encourage the church in Corinth about the subject of temptation he says, "No temptation has overtaken you except such as is common to man; but God *is* faithful, who will not allow you to be tempted beyond what you are able, but with the temptation will also make the way of escape, that you may be able to bear it." 1 Corinthians 10:13 (NKJV)

Whenever you pray and sing praise to the Lord in adversity; in the context of this book if anyone refuses to be sad but rejoices in temptation, test or trial God has no option other than to bring deliverance or victory for anything in which you have expressed your joy in faith. By praying and praising the Lord in crisis, in other words by expressing joy in adversity you are offering Him advance payment for hearing your prayer. The point is that man will often fail you, even when you have paid in advance when they are offered an improved deal. However, the Lord, will always honour His word because He is faithful as Paul wrote to the Corinthians in the quotation above.

Trust the faithfulness of God by praising Him or be joyful at all times or in any circumstance knowing that God will not permit you to be tempted beyond what you can bear and He will never disappoint you. For more details about prayer and praise read my book ***"The Power for your Zero Hour, Praising the Lord, even in Adversity"*** you will find out what happened to Paul and Silas after they had prayed and sang praises to God in their zero hour.

The Devil or your enemy's intention will be to harm you with any situation you have been pushed into, but with prayer and praise that will turn to be for your good because the Lord will turn it to be your training ground and the base for your better future.

Examples

In one of his greatest temptations, Joseph's brothers out of jealousy wanted to get rid of him because of his dreams and also the love their father had for him:

We read from Gen 37:18-20 (NKJV)

Now when they saw him afar off, even before he came near them, they conspired against him to kill him. Then they said to one another, "Look, this dreamer is coming! Come therefore, let us now kill him and cast him into some pit; and we shall say, 'Some wild beast has devoured him.' We shall see what will become of his dreams!"

God turned their evil intentions into a blessing when he became Prime Minister, the second in command in Egypt and so in Genesis chapter 50 when his brothers were trying to blame one another for their actions, after he had revealed himself to them in verse 20 he said:

"But as for you, you meant evil against me; but God meant it for good, in order to bring it about as *it is* this day, to save many people alive." (NKJV)

For this reason as you read this book, I entreat you to be joyful in whatever situation you find yourself it is one of the powerful ways to face temptation.

In another supportive lesson, James also said, "Consider it pure joy, my brothers, whenever you face trials of many kinds" I want us to have a deeper study into these words of James as it offers great help in the subject.

These words of the Apostle taken from James 1:2, seems to me to be contradictory. Given that the Book of James deals with the principles of Christian living and specifically cites temptation, it is highly relevant to the theme of this book. However, what are we to make of James' advice to us as Christians, find joy in difficulty and pain? Certainly, this kind of advice would not make sense to anyone who is not a believer! In fact, I must admit that even to some Christians being happy in the face of temptation would not be easy advice to accept.

The Book of James is full of exhortations and admonitions about the way we are to conduct ourselves as followers of Jesus Christ in times of temptation. It was written by James the brother of Jesus and the leader of the first-century Church in

Jerusalem, to advise the Christians spreading the Gospel to the Gentiles outside Jerusalem; because of the persecution, they faced.

The major theme of the Book of James is that 'true faith' is in living an active life of obedience and righteousness in Christ. So, we can take it that James 1:2 is an exhortation to literally approach the many afflictions we face as a joyful opportunity. Given how difficult and painful temptation and its consequences can be, it begs the question: 'what is it about temptation that we should rejoice in?' In answer to the question, James 1:3 explains: "because you know that the testing of your faith develops perseverance. Perseverance must finish its work so that you may be mature and complete, not lacking anything."

James 1:12 also says:

"God blesses those who patiently endure testing." NLT

I believe that facing and being able to persevere when our faith is tested, in this instance by temptations, is an example of 'true faith 'at work. "True faith' is not just about claiming a belief in God, it's about repentance, actively turning from sin; and relying totally on the promises of God for our lives.

I believe that our having joy in the face of trials, is about rejoicing in the opportunity temptations present us to continually 'choose' Christ, to resist temptation and live a life worthy of the Lord, a life that pleases him in every way, a fruitful life in which we grow in the knowledge of God (see Colossians 1:10)

When we are able to turn temptation into opportunity, we walk worthy, we have escaped temptation and we have right standing with Him. In Luke 21:36 our Lord Jesus Christ says:

"Watch therefore, and pray always that you may be counted worthy to escape all these things that will come to pass and to stand before the Son of Man." (NKJV)

The Bible even tells us that our 'afflictions' are supposed to work for us as Paul said: For our light affliction, which is but for a moment, is working for us a far more exceeding and eternal weight of glory, 2 Corinthians 4:17 (NKJV)

We should be able to endure 'our light afflictions', knowing that this too shall pass, and being reassured by the promise of the word of God which says, "No temptation has seized you except what is common to man. And God is faithful; he will not let you be tempted beyond what you can bear. But when you are tempted, he will also provide a way out so that you can stand up under it." 1 Corinthians 10:13

The Lord has planned a way out! I am not trying to understate the real and present dangers temptation, tests and trials present. What I am saying is that as with everything else in our Christian life, when faced with it, we must:

"Look unto Jesus, the author and finisher of our faith, who for the joy set before him, endured the cross, despising the shame." Hebrews 12:2

We overcome everything that would seek to derail us from the purposes and promises of God, through the blood of the Lamb and the word of our testimony. Revelation 12:11

Our Lord Himself says:

"When they call on me, I will answer; I will be with them in trouble. I will rescue them and honour them. I will satisfy them with a long life and give them my salvation." Psalm 91:15-16, NLT

***

Conclusion

Always remember that temptation is an ever present part of the life of a Christian, note that temptation (test and trial from God and temptation that come from the Devil) can be successfully managed by the grace of God. Therefore as we read in the early stage of this book I also want you to note, as I prepare to end that temptation will come irrespective of your spiritual backgrounds, your relationship with God, and whether or not you deserve the punishment of temptation or the test you must always prepare.

I pray that this guide becomes a useful and well-used resource, to help you turn the threat of temptation into an opportunity to move into a higher level in your life. When you do, you will be blessed as the bible says, "God blesses those who patiently endure testing. Afterward they will receive the crown of life that God has promised to those who love him" James 1:12, NLT

Although the object of our faith is unseen; have faith and confidence in God to endure the testing and God's promise and provision will be yours. Never underestimate the effect of temptation it can cause you to doubt God's goodness which can affect your relationship with Him as it did to Adam and Eve in the Garden of Eden

No matter how difficult it may be you must resist and never be drawn to it for like David, falling into the Devil's temptation can have a lasting consequence that can affect your generations after you

Whatever happens to you in life, even in adversity or in your zero hour be stable be at peace, be joyful and victory will always be yours.

Never run from God because of temptation rather let it draw you to Him for there is an end to every temptation.

Like Jesus Christ, the example of our faith whenever you face any situation in your life use the word for the word will always produce result. With the word, you will overcome any temptation, test or trial you may face in life

"For this reason we also thank God without ceasing, because when you received the word of God which you heard from us, you welcomed it not *as the word of men, but as it is in truth, the word of God, which also effectively works in you who believe."* 1 Thessalonians 2:13 (NKJV)

But he who looks into the perfect law of liberty and continues in it, and is not a forgetful hearer but a doer of the work, this one will be blessed in what he does. James 1:25 (NKJV)

If God test you and ask you to give Him anything even if it is your only one be willing to give or offer it to Him in joy knowing that He who gave you the power to whatever you possess is also able to provide, for God loves a cheerful giver.

Be able to identify the source of any temptation that comes your way

For now understand that the simplest way to distinguish the test/trial that comes from God, and the temptation which is from the Devil's is that – at the end of the Lord's test stands righteousness and divine approval, not condemnation. While at the end of every instance of Satan's temptations, is evil, sin and if we continue in it unrepentant, ultimately damnation! To be tempted is not sin but to give into it is.

***

Other Publications by Pastor David Amoah

Lead Us Not Into Temptation

Be Ye Transformed

Stay Connected To Christ

Your Future Is In Your Hand

The Power For Your Zero Hour

Guidelines for Preachers and Teachers of God's Word

***

www.ingramcontent.com/pod-product-compliance
Lightning Source LLC
Chambersburg PA
CBHW071502080526
44587CB00014B/2187